Writer's Companion
Support and Practice for Writing
Grade 5

Harcourt School Publishers

www.harcourtschool.com

ISBN 10: 0-15-367076-2
ISBN 13: 978-0-15-367076-3

1 2 3 4 5 6 7 8 9 10 022 17 16 14 13 12 11 10 09 08 07

Contents

Introduction **5**

UNIT 1

WRITER'S CRAFT:
VOICE AND
WORD CHOICE

LESSON 1 Sensory Details **8**
Literature Model Rope Burn
Student Model Character Description

LESSON 2 Writer's Viewpoint **14**
Literature Model Line Drive
Student Model Autobiographical Composition

LESSON 3 Writing a Strong Lead **20**
Literature Model Evren Ozan, Musician
Student Model Autobiographical Narrative

Test Prep **LESSON 4 Review/Extended Written Response** **26**
Literature Model The Daring Nellie Bly: America's Star Reporter
Student Model News Article

Test Prep **LESSON 5 Writing Test Practice** **32**

UNIT 2

WRITER'S CRAFT:
IDEAS AND
ORGANIZATION

LESSON 6 Elaborating with Examples **38**
Literature Model The Night of San Juan
Student Model Personal Response Paragraph

LESSON 7 Staying on Topic **44**
Literature Model When the Circus Came to Town
Student Model Journal Entry

LESSON 8 Time-Order Words **50**
Literature Model When Washington Crossed the Delaware
Student Model Biography

Test Prep **LESSON 9 Review/Extended Written Response** **56**
Literature Model Leonardo's Horse
Student Model Summary

Test Prep **LESSON 10 Writing Test Practice** **62**

UNIT 3

WRITER'S CRAFT:
SENTENCE FLUENCY
AND CONVENTIONS

LESSON 11 Sentence Beginnings **68**
Literature Model Sailing Home: A Story of a Childhood at Sea
Student Model Descriptive Paragraph

LESSON 12 Making Clear Comparisons and Contrasts **74**
Literature Model Ultimate Field Trip 3: Wading into Marine Biology
Student Model Compare-and-Contrast Composition

LESSON 13 Using Precise Nouns and Verbs **80**
Literature Model Stormalong
Student Model Descriptive Paragraph

Test Prep **LESSON 14 Review/Extended Written Response** **86**
Literature Model A Drop of Water
Student Model Cause-and-Effect Paragraph

Test Prep **LESSON 15 Writing Test Practice** **92**

UNIT 4
WRITER'S CRAFT:
VOICE AND
WORD CHOICE

LESSON 16 Sensory Details 98
Literature Model How Anansi Gave the World Stories
Student Model Narrative Paragraph

LESSON 17 Creating Specific Voices 104
Literature Model Nothing Ever Happens on 90th Street
Student Model Skit

LESSON 18 Vivid Words and Phrases 110
Literature Model Project Mulberry
Student Model Suspense Story

Test Prep **LESSON 19 Review/Extended Written Response** 116
Literature Model Inventing the Future: A Photobiography of Thomas Alva Edison
Student Model Letter of Request

Test Prep **LESSON 20 Writing Test Practice** 122

UNIT 5
WRITER'S CRAFT:
SENTENCE
FLUENCY AND
ORGANIZATION

LESSON 21 Sentences with Facts and Reasons 128
Literature Model Interrupted Journey: Saving Endangered Sea Turtles
Student Model Persuasive Letter

LESSON 22 Varying Sentence Type and Length 134
Literature Model The Power of W.O.W!
Student Model Persuasive Paragraph

LESSON 23 Create a Memorable Ending 140
Literature Model Any Small Goodness: A Novel of the Barrio
Student Model Poem

Test Prep **LESSON 24 Review/Extended Written Response** 146
Literature Model Chester Cricket's Pigeon Ride
Student Model Narrative Composition

Test Prep **LESSON 25 Writing Test Practice** 152

UNIT 6
WRITER'S CRAFT:
IDEAS AND
CONVENTIONS

LESSON 26 More on Topics and Details 158
Literature Model Lewis and Clark
Student Model Paragraph of Explanation

LESSON 27 Facts Versus Opinion 164
Literature Model Klondike Kate
Student Model Paragraph of Historical Information

LESSON 28 Putting Ideas in Sequence 170
Literature Model The Top of the World: Climbing Mount Everest
Student Model How-to Paragraph

Test Prep **LESSON 29 Review/Extended Written Response** 176
Literature Model The Man Who Went to the Far Side of the Moon
Student Model Essay of Explanation

Test Prep **LESSON 30 Writing Test Practice** 182

CONVENTIONS

Writer's Grammar Guide 188
Proofreading Strategies 200
Proofreader's Marks 201

WRITER'S
RESOURCES

Writing Across the Curriculum/Presentation 202
Writer's Glossary of Terms 206
Rubrics 207

Introduction

Writing is a way of sharing your ideas. Of course, you share ideas when you talk with others, too. When you write, however, you end up with a lasting record. Writing captures your thoughts just as a photograph captures your appearance.

This book will give you the skills, strategies, tips, and models you need to write easily and effectively. Let's start with an introduction to the writing process and some ongoing strategies.

The Writing Process

One big difference between writing and talking is the element of time. When you write, you have time to plan what you'll say, say it, and then make changes until it's just right. This is your writing process. Though there is no one correct way to write, many writers go through the following writing stages.

Prewriting

In this stage, you prepare to write. You plan what you will write by choosing a topic, identifying your audience, brainstorming and researching ideas, and organizing information.

Drafting

Next you follow your Prewriting plan to write a first draft. Don't expect your writing to be perfect—just let the sentences flow according to your plan.

Revising

Now you have the opportunity to improve your writing. As you edit, you will look for ways to make your writing clearer and stronger. You might edit by yourself or with a partner or group.

Proofreading

In this final stage of editing, you check for errors in grammar, spelling, capitalization, and punctuation. Then you make a clean, final copy.

Publishing

Finally, you decide how you will share your writing with your audience. You might create a newsletter, present a multimedia presentation, mail a letter, or assemble a class book.

Writer's Craft and Writing Traits

You've probably heard the phrase "arts and crafts" used to describe handmade items like quilts or pottery. Craftspeople make works of art that are both beautiful and useful. You can think of writing as a craft, too. Instead of using pieces of cloth to make a quilt, you use words to build a story, a letter, or a poem.

A key part of developing your craft is recognizing good writing. This web shows some of the traits you should look for in a piece of writing.

The Traits of Good Writing

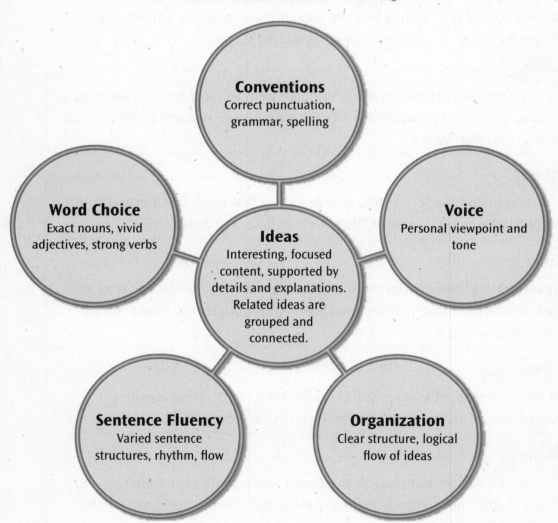

Conventions
Correct punctuation, grammar, spelling

Word Choice
Exact nouns, vivid adjectives, strong verbs

Ideas
Interesting, focused content, supported by details and explanations. Related ideas are grouped and connected.

Voice
Personal viewpoint and tone

Sentence Fluency
Varied sentence structures, rhythm, flow

Organization
Clear structure, logical flow of ideas

Traits Checklist

Questions like these can help you improve your skills. Every time you answer "yes" to one of these questions, you recognize the strength of your writing.

☑ FOCUS/IDEAS	Is my writing clear and focused? Do I keep my purpose and audience in mind? Have I supported my ideas with interesting details and reasons?
☑ ORGANIZATION	Do my ideas have a logical flow? Is my beginning effective? What about my ending? Does each paragraph focus on one idea? Do I use transition words to tie ideas together?
☑ VOICE	Does the writing sound like I wrote it? Have I added personal touches? Have I shown that I care about what I am saying?
☑ WORD CHOICE	Do I use energetic words that create interest? Have I used strong verbs, precise nouns, and vivid adjectives?
☑ SENTENCE FLUENCY	Do I use different kinds of sentences? Do I use the best sentence structure for my ideas?
☑ CONVENTIONS	Are my spelling, grammar, and punctuation correct?

Writer's Companion
Introduction

Name _____

Identify: Sensory Details

Sensory details help readers see, hear, smell, taste, or feel what a writer is describing.

A. Read this passage. Notice how the writer uses sensory details.

> ## Literature Model
>
> After gym, I went to my locker to get my lunch. As I was dialing my combination , I heard someone say, "You're not too crazy about rope-climbing, are you?"
>
> I turned to see a dark-skinned boy looking at me through thick glasses.
>
> "Actually, I hate rope-climbing," I admitted. "How did you guess?"
>
> "You looked like you were going to pass out when Mr. Reynolds was talking about it," explained the boy. He was wearing black jeans and a bright yellow T-shirt with a picture of a lizard coming out of its pocket.
>
> —from *Rope Burn*
> by Jan Siebold

B. Look for sensory details in the literature model.
1. Draw a box around the words that describe what you can see.
2. Circle the words that describe what you can hear.

C. What words could you add that would appeal to the sense of touch? Include them in a sentence that you could add to the passage.

_____

_____

_____

_____

_____

© Harcourt

Name _____

Explore: Sensory Details

Sensory details appeal to the senses of sight, sound, smell, taste, and touch.
They help give readers a first-hand experience of what a writer is describing.
They also help readers understand a writer's thoughts and feelings.

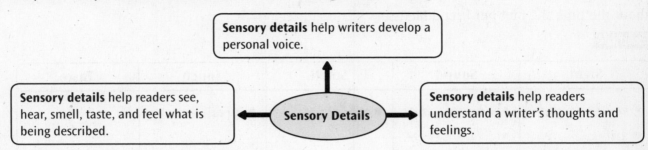

Sensory details help writers develop a personal voice.

Sensory details help readers see, hear, smell, taste, and feel what is being described.

Sensory Details

Sensory details help readers understand a writer's thoughts and feelings.

A. **Read each sentence. Then circle the sense that the underlined details appeal to most.**

Example The <u>frigid</u> water <u>numbed</u> my feet as I walked along the beach.

        sight   sound   (touch)

1. The smoky campfire gave our clothes an <u>air</u> of <u>burnt</u> <u>wood</u>.

        touch   sound   smell

2. A <u>toothy</u> <u>grin</u> <u>spread</u> <u>across</u> <u>her</u> <u>face</u> when she heard the good news.

        sight   sound   touch

3. My finger <u>traced</u> the <u>chipped</u> and <u>cracked</u> <u>stone</u> <u>surface</u> of the statue.

        sight   sound   touch

B. **Read the passage. Then answer the questions.**

> I grabbed the rope and slowly started to climb. My hands were tender from practicing all weekend. My gym shorts were more slippery than the jeans I had been wearing.

1. Underline the sensory details in the passage.

2. To what sense does each detail appeal?

_____

_____

3. What do the sensory details tell you about rope climbing?

_____

_____

_____

© Harcourt

Name _____

Use: Sensory Details

A **character description** gives a clear picture of what someone is like. Before you write a character description, make a chart of sensory details that come to mind when you think of that person. Here is how one student started to brainstorm about the time she met her friend Melissa.

Example

Sight	Sound	Smell	Touch	Taste
• wide-eyed • purple • bouncing • wiggled • wildly	• chattering • "n-n-n-no" • quieted	• chlorine	• wet	

A. Think about someone you consider a good friend. Write his or her name on the line. Then fill out the chart with the sensory details that come to mind when you think of that person.

Name of Friend _____

Sight	Sound	Smell	Touch	Taste

B. Use information from your chart to write a draft of a character description about your friend. Do your writing on another sheet of paper.

Name _____

The Parts of a Character Description

A good **character description** paints a vivid portrait of what someone is like. It uses sensory details to give readers a first-hand impression of that person. Here is an example of a character description written by a fifth-grade student. As you read, think about how the student organized it. Then answer the questions.

Student Model

Getting Warm
by Tina

Melissa and I met at the indoor pool, while waiting in line for the high dive. The air was thick with chlorine. She was wet and cold. She was the only one in line who wasn't shouting at the boy who was frozen with fear on the board. Melissa was wide-eyed with excitement. I had never seen her before even though I went to the pool almost every day. The anticipation of jumping off the high dive clearly thrilled her.

I offered to get a towel if she held my place in line.

"N-n-n-no," she said. "I have a better idea."

Melissa started bouncing on her toes and then wildly wiggling her arms over her head. The kids quieted and looked at her. She didn't seem to care. She was just getting warm.

> **Introduce** the character in the first sentence.

> Choose an appropriate **organization**—order of events, order of importance, etc.

> **Develop** your character description by using sensory details.

> **Use** different types of sentences to help make your writing interesting.

1. Underline the sentence that introduces the character.
2. Draw a circle around the sentence that seems to be out of order. Then draw an arrow to the place where you think this sentence will make more sense.
3. Find the sensory details in the passage. Write at least one example of each.

Sight: _____   Sound: _____

Smell: _____   Touch: _____

4. What else do the sensory details tell you about Melissa?

_____

Name _____

Evaluate a Character Description

When you evaluate a character description, ask yourself how well it helped you
picture the person that it describes.

Now evaluate the Student Model. Put a check in the box next to each thing
the writer did well. If you do not think the writer did a good job, do not check
the box.

☐ The writer introduced the character in the first sentence.
☐ The writer organized the character description in an appropriate way.
☐ The writer developed the character description by using sensory details
☐ The writer used different types of sentences.

Writer's Grammar
Declarative and Interrogative Sentences

A **declarative sentence** makes a statement. It ends with a period.
Example The fireworks looked like flowers blooming in the night sky.

An **interrogative sentence** asks a question. It ends with a question mark.
Example Who painted the purple circles on the ceiling?

**Read each sentence. Add the correct end punctuation. Then tell whether
it is a declarative or interrogative sentence. Circle your answer.**

1. Whoever knocked the cans off the shelf made quite a racket___

       declarative   interrogative

2. Have you ever scraped your knee on the sidewalk___

       declarative   interrogative

3. Did you notice how well she played the piano___

       declarative   interrogative

4. The dark clouds overhead threatened rain___

       declarative   interrogative

Name _____

Revise: Replacing Plain Words

One thing the writer might have done better was to use sensory details instead of ordinary words. Sensory details make writing more vivid, descriptive, and enjoyable to read. Here is an example of how a sentence from the Student Model could be improved.

Example She was wet and cold.

Water drizzled from her ponytail as she shivered and rubbed her arms for warmth.

A. Revise these sentences. Replace the plain words with vivid sensory details.

1. Melissa was wide-eyed with excitement.

_____

_____

2. "N-n-n-no," she said.

_____

_____

3. The kids quieted and looked at her.

_____

_____

4. She didn't seem to care.

_____

_____

Word Bank

curly
focused
glared
ignore
intensely
shiver
soaked
sputter
_____
_____

B. Revise the character description you wrote on page 10. Replace plain words with vivid sensory details. Use another sheet of paper.

Writer's Companion • UNIT 1
Lesson 1 *Sensory Details*

Name _____

Identify: Writer's Viewpoint

A **writer's viewpoint** is how he or she thinks or feels about something. Writers often use sensory details and personal details to express their viewpoint to their readers.

A. Read the following passage. Notice how the writer expresses her viewpoint.

Literature Model

Growing up the oldest sister of three brothers doesn't always make you a tomboy, but it helps. And having a mom who would rather punt a football than sew a quilt sets the stage for some great sports memories, too. Obviously, no one ever told me that girls couldn't play baseball or ride a boy's bike or wrestle Indian-style. I could smack a grimy hardball across the fence with the best of the neighborhood boys—and I was just a skinny, short girl with glasses. Mom taught us—her sons and daughters—how to do all those things.

—from Line Drive
by Tanya West Dean

B. Find places in the passage where the writer expresses her viewpoint.
1. Underline words that express the writer's viewpoint about her mother's influence on her.
2. Put a box around words the writer uses to express her viewpoint about her brothers' influence.
3. Circle a second sensory detail that expresses the writer's actions and feelings about playing baseball.
4. What personal details help you know the writer's viewpoint about herself and her family?

_____

_____

C. The writer says she has a mother "who would rather punt a football than sew a quilt." How might the writer's viewpoint have been different if she had a mother who would rather sew a quilt than punt a football?

_____

_____

_____

Name _____

Explore: Writer's Viewpoint

Vivid sensory details help writers express their viewpoint. Personal experiences and details also can help writers express their thoughts and feelings about a topic.

Sensory Details: how it looked, felt, sounded, and so on. → Viewpoint ← Personal Details: what I did, how I felt, and so on.

A. **Read each sentence. Then write the words that express the writer's viewpoint.**

> **Example** When I heard the terrible news that the Buzzards had won the championship, I sighed and slowly walked home, dragging my feet the whole way.

terrible, sighed, slowly walked, dragging my feet the whole way

1. When I was young, I would spring up and sprint outside as soon as the first ray of sunshine broke into my room.

_____

_____

2. I was concerned about the deafening level of noise pollution, so I wrote a letter to the mayor.

_____

_____

3. My grandfather warned me that I should never let anyone fool me into giving up my dreams.

_____

_____

B. **Read the passage from *Line Drive*. Then answer the questions.**

My heart started to beat all the way into my ears. As I took a couple of practice swings, I realized that I was all lined up to be a dead girl.

1. Underline the words that show the writer's viewpoint.

2. What is writer's viewpoint at the moment she steps up to bat? Describe it in your own words.

_____

_____

Name _____

Use: Writer's Viewpoint

If you ever wrote about your own life, you have written an **autobiographical composition.** When you express your viewpoint about your life, you let the reader know your feelings and opinions. Here is how one student started to think about an important event in his life.

Example

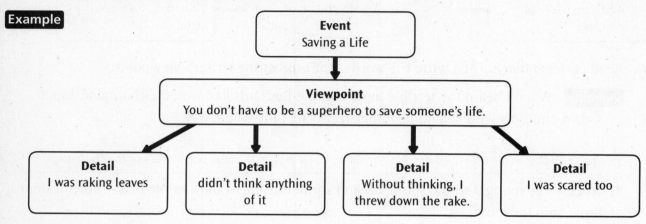

A. Think about an important event in your life that taught you something about yourself. Then fill out the organizer with your viewpoint and some personal details.

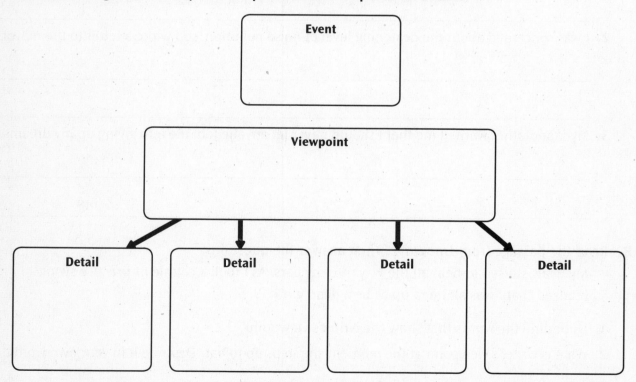

B. Use the information from your organizer to draft a paragraph about an important event in your life that taught you something. Do your writing on another sheet of paper.

© Harcourt

Name _____

The Parts of an Autobiographical Composition

An **autobiographical composition** tells about an event or events in the writer's life. Here is an example of an autobiographical composition written by a fifth-grade student. As you read, think about how the student organized it. Also think about how the writer used sensory and personal details. Then answer the questions.

Student Model

DRAFT

Just a Normal Hero
by Colin

You don't have to be a superhero to save someone's life. One day I was raking leaves when I heard a loud metallic bang. At first I didn't think anything of it. But as I continued raking I thought I could hear a strange cry. I looked through the bushes and saw a man pinned under the wheel of a truck. He must have been working under it when it fell on top of him. Without thinking, I threw down the rake, ran inside, and told my sister to call 9-1-1. He looked scared. I ran back outside and knelt next to the man. I held his hand and told him help was on the way. I was scared, too, but I tried not to show it.

> **Introduce** the viewpoint in the first sentence.

> **Develop** your ideas using personal details. Use first-person point of view.

> **Organize** the events in chronological order.

> **Use** sensory details to help readers share the experience in a first-hand way.

1. Underline the sentence in which the writer introduces his viewpoint.

2. Draw a box around the personal details that the writer uses to develop his viewpoint.

3. Circle sensory details that help readers see, hear, and feel the experience.

Name _____

Evaluate an Autobiographical Composition

When you evaluate an autobiographical composition, ask yourself if you understand how the writer feels about the events he describes.

Now evaluate the Student Model. Put a check in the box next to each thing the writer did well. If you do not think the writer did a good job, do not check the box.

- ☐ The writer introduced the viewpoint in the first sentence.
- ☐ The writer developed his ideas with personal details.
- ☐ The writer used sensory details to help readers share the experience.
- ☐ The writer organized the events in chronological order.

Writer's Grammar
Exclamatory Sentences

An exclamatory sentence expresses strong feeling. It ends with an exclamation point. Exclamatory sentences help writers make their writing lively and interesting.

Example That was a good performance.

What an amazing show!

Read the declarative sentences below. Then rewrite each sentence to make it an exclamatory sentence that expresses stronger feeling.

Example I liked the movie.

It was the best movie I'd ever seen!

1. My grandmother's tamales taste very good.

_____

2. I thanked the firefighter three times.

_____

3. I couldn't believe what I was seeing.

_____

4. The sculpture was very realistic.

_____

Name _____

Revise: Adding Personal Details

One thing the writer could have done better was to use personal details. They would have made his viewpoint even clearer. Adding personal details also could have made the writing more entertaining. Here is how a sentence from the Student Model could be improved.

Example   I was raking leaves when I heard a loud metallic bang.

I was raking leaves for my parents, like I do every Saturday morning in the fall, when I heard a loud metallic bang.

A. Revise these by adding personal details that the writer might have used. Use the Word Bank to help you.

Word Bank
chores
garbage
dinner
dishes
soccer
  league
feel
thunder-
  storms
hurricanes
pancake
strawberry
  shortcake
_____
_____

1. I have chores to do at home.

_____

_____

_____

2. I play on a sports team.

_____

_____

3. I do not like certain kinds of weather.

_____

_____

4. My grandmother is a good cook.

_____

_____

B. Revise the draft of an autobiographical composition you wrote on page 16 by adding personal details. Do your writing on another sheet of paper.

Name _____

Identify: Writing A Strong Lead

A **lead** is the first sentence or paragraph of a piece of writing. A **strong lead** sparks readers' attention and makes them want to continue reading. Descriptive words, sensory details, quotations, and interrogative sentences all can help make a strong lead.

A. Read this strong lead from an interview with ten-year-old musician Evren Ozan. Notice how the writer uses descriptive words to make the reader want to read further.

Literature Model

Although artists in the music circle tend to describe Evren as the "Native American Flute Prodigy," "An Old Soul Returned to the People," and the "Future of Native American Music," I found him to be an exceptional ten-year-old who is smart, talented, creative, resourceful, inspiring, and on the whole, awesome.

—from *Evren Ozan, Musician*
by Harsha Viswanathan

B. Find words that catch readers' interest.
   1. Underline the words the writer uses in the lead to catch the reader's attention.
   2. The writer uses quotations to show the reader what others think about Evren. Put a box around the quotations that are used to spark readers' attention.

C. What other words would you choose to use to spark readers' interest in Evren Ozan? Write them on the lines below.

_____

_____

_____

_____

Name _____

Explore: Writing A Strong Lead

A strong lead grabs readers' attention and makes them curious enough to continue reading.

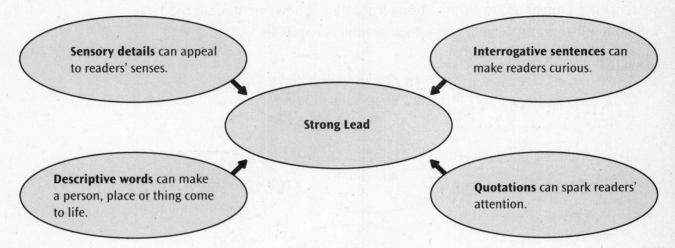

A. Read each pair of lead sentences below. Underline the sentence that is the stronger lead.

Example   Cars that run on ethanol might become more popular in the future.

Do you think you will ever drive a car that runs on corn?

1. Exhausted, Jorge stumbled into a clearing in the rain forest and couldn't believe his eyes.
    After hiking on the trail for two hours Jorge arrived at the ruins.

2. What weighs a ton and looks like a hippopotamus with flippers?
    A manatee is a large mammal that lives in shallow coastal waters.

3. Many vivid images come to mind when thinking about winter.
    Picture warming your hands around a hot mug of sweet apple cider.

4. With one second left in the game, the crowd hushed as I stepped toward the free throw line.
    With one second left in the game, I knew I couldn't afford to miss the free throw.

B. Rewrite the following sentence to make a stronger lead.

I had fun this weekend with my family at the natural history museum.

_____

_____

_____

Name _____

Use: Writing A Strong Lead

An **autobiographical narrative** tells about an event in the writer's life. Before you write an autobiographical narrative, brainstorm the details and type of sentences you might use to write a strong lead. Here is how one student used a web to brainstorm the lead of her autobiographical narrative.

Example

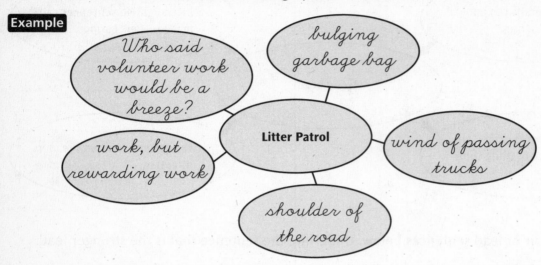

Who said volunteer work would be a breeze?

bulging garbage bag

work, but rewarding work

Litter Patrol

wind of passing trucks

shoulder of the road

A. Think about an event in your life that made you feel that you had accomplished something. Write the name of the event in the center of the web. Then use the web to brainstorm details and sentences for a strong lead.

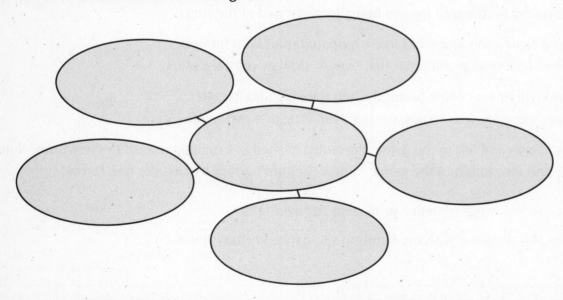

B. Use the information from your web to draft an autobiographical narrative about a time when you felt that you accomplished something. Make sure you have a strong lead to grab readers' attention. Do your writing on another sheet of paper.

© Harcourt

Name _____

The Parts of an Autobiographical Narrative

In an autobiographical narrative, a writer describes something that happened in his or her life. Here is an example of an autobiographical narrative written by a fifth-grade student. As you read, think about how the student organized it. Then answer the questions.

Student Model

**Litter Patrol
by Tanya**

There I stood, on the shoulder of the road, with a stick in one hand and a bulging garbage bag in the other. Who said volunteer work would be a breeze? The only breeze I felt all day was the wind of passing trucks. Litter patrol was work, but it was rewarding work.

The day began when I put a soda can into the bag. I don't like soda very much. Then I took a couple steps and picked up a tattered magazine. Next I pulled a plastic bag from a shrub.

As I worked, I started to think about what I could do to make my town cleaner. The next thing I knew, two hours had passed. I turned around. The shoulder of the road was trash free!

Begin with a **strong lead** that will make readers want to read more.

Make the topic and setting clear to your readers.

Develop your ideas by using sensory details and descriptive words.

Organize events in chronological order. Use transition words such as *first*, *then* and *next*.

Use complete sentences. Each must have a subject and a predicate.

1. Which is the lead sentence? Underline it.
2. Circle words in the first paragraph that describe the setting.
3. Which detail does not relate to the topic and seems out of place? Cross it out.
4. What transition words help show the chronological order of events? Write them.

_____

5. Which details help grab readers' attention? Write them below.

_____

_____

_____

_____

© Harcourt

Name _____

Evaluate an Autobiographical Narrative

When you evaluate an autobiographical narrative, ask yourself whether it has a strong lead that draws the reader in and introduces the topic. Also ask yourself whether the writer uses vivid details that are organized in chronological order.

Now evaluate the Student Model. Put a check in the box next to each thing the writer did well. If you do not think the writer did a good job, do not check the box.

☐ The writer introduced the topic and setting with a strong lead that made readers want to read more.

☐ The writer developed his or her ideas using sensory details and descriptive words.

☐ The writer organized events in chronological order and used transition words to make the order clear to the readers.

☐ The writer used complete sentences that have both a subject and predicate.

Writer's Grammar
Subjects and Predicates

A complete sentence expresses a complete thought. It has a subject and a predicate. The **subject** is the person, place, thing, or idea that the sentence is about. The **predicate** is the word or words that tell what the subject is or does.

Example <u>Subjects</u>   <u>Predicates</u>

The recycling center is brand-new.

My grandmother lifts weights at the gym.

For each sentence below, underline the subject once and the predicate twice.

1. The astronauts trained for years.

2. Gabriella and Ted volunteered at the animal shelter for the summer.

3. Tallahassee is the capital of Florida.

4. Honesty and courage are two positive traits.

5. The exhausted climber was approaching the summit of the mountain.

© Harcourt

Name _____

Revise: Using Descriptive Words

One thing the writer could have done better was to use descriptive words.
These words can help paint a colorful picture of the events that the writer is
describing. Here is how a sentence from the Student Model could be improved
using descriptive words.

Example   The only breeze I felt all day was the wind of passing trucks.

The only breezes I felt all day were the gritty gusts

kicked up by the trucks that roared by.

A. Revise these sentences by using descriptive words. Use the Word Bank to help you.

   1. Litter patrol was work, but it was rewarding work.

_____

_____

   2. The day began when I put a soda can into the bag.

_____

_____

   3. Next I pulled a plastic bag from a shrub.

_____

_____

   4. I turned around.

_____

_____

B. Revise the autobiographical narrative you wrote for page 22. Be sure to use
descriptive words. Do your writing on another sheet of paper.

> **Word
> Bank**
>
> branches
> crumpled
> crushed
> empty
> filthy
> remains
> satisfying
> slowly
> tiring
> _____
> _____

© Harcourt

Name _____

Review: Writer's Craft

Personal and sensory details help writers express their viewpoint, which is how they think and feel about a topic. Sensory details can also give readers a first-hand experience of something. Like quotations, descriptive words, and questions, sensory details help writers create strong leads for their writing.

A. Read the passage below. Notice how the writer uses descriptive words to express a feeling of excitement.

Literature Model

Soon Nellie Bly was the *World's* star stunt reporter, responsible for coming up with her own great story ideas.

One sleepless night she had an extraordinary idea. She would break the fictional record of Phileas Fogg, who went around the world in eighty days in Jules Verne's popular novel.

In the late 1800s it took many months to travel around the world. Boats were late, trains were slow, and connections were often missed. But Nellie checked the timetables and was convinced she could beat Fogg's record. Her editor was doubtful . . . . But Nellie was determined . . . . Besides, if the *World* wouldn't send her, she'd simply find another newspaper that would.

—from *The Daring Nellie Bly: America's Star Reporter*
by Bonnie Christensen

B. Find sensory details and personal viewpoint.
1. Underline words that help you know the writer's viewpoint about Nellie Bly.
2. Put a box around sensory details that give readers a picture of Nellie Bly.
3. Double underline details about what Nellie did that help readers understand what she was like.

C. What could you add or change to make this an even better lead for the selection? On the lines below, tell what you would do.

_____

_____

_____

Name _____

Review: Writer's Craft

Personal and sensory details can help writers express their voice. These details also can help create a strong lead for a piece of writing.

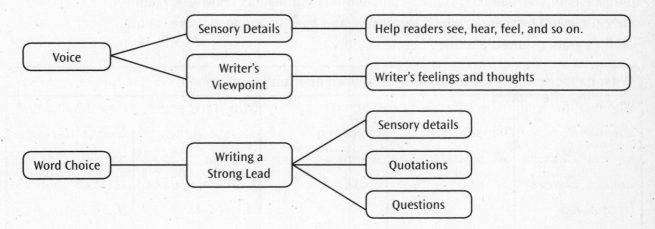

A. After reading the passage below, underline the sensory details and descriptive words that help bring the scene to life for the reader. Then answer the question.

> While most people are sound asleep, dreaming of tropical paradises in the warmth and comfort of their homes, Marcia Gomez is braving the bone-chilling winds and icy waters off the Alaskan coast.

B. Read each sentence below. Rewrite each one, using sensory details, questions, or quotations to make it a stronger lead.

Example The Eagles won the championship last night.

Cheered on by the roar of their fans, the Clarkstown Eagles soared to victory last night.

1. We did not know who was knocking on the door.

_____

_____

2. I was nervous to climb the climbing wall.

_____

_____

© Harcourt

Review: Writer's Craft

Before you write a **news article** about something that happened in your community, think about the sensory details you could use to make the scene come alive for your readers. Those details should help readers know *when* and *where* the event happened, *why* it happened, and *how* it happened. Here is how one fifth grader started planning her news story.

What happened: Bears came walking into town one Sunday afternoon.				
Who was involved	Where it happened	When it happened	Why it happened	How it happened
Glenville police, Glenda Curtis, Officer Menasha	*Glenville*	*Sunday night*	*Bears are losing their natural habitat*	*Bears walked down Main Street and then returned to woods*

A. Read the lead sentences below. Then follow the directions.

While most people are sound asleep, safe and warm in their homes and dreaming of tropical paradises, Marcia Gomez is braving the bone-chilling winds and icy waters off the Alaskan coast. She works on a fishing boat, laboring long hours to bring in the fresh fish that graces our tables. It's a difficult life, with long hours, physical discomfort, and always the chance of not making a good catch. Why does she do it? "I love it," she says. "My family has fished for generations. It's in our blood."

1. Underline the lead sentence.
2. What details grab your attention in that sentence? Circle them.
3. What words tell where the story takes place? Box them.
4. What sensory details are included in the passage?

_____

B. Add two sentences to this passage. Use sensory details to make it come alive.

_____

_____

_____

© Harcourt

Name _____

The Parts of a News Article

A **news article** tells the facts about an event that has happened recently. Here is an example of a news article written by a fifth-grade student. As you read, think about how the student organized it. Then answer the questions.

Student Model

DRAFT

Rojas Rides to City Hall
by Kimberly

Fifth grader Andy Rojas rode his bicycle to City Hall and presented a petition to the city council requesting more bicycle lanes in the neighborhood surrounding Goodwin Elementary School. "More bicycle lanes," Andy said, "would make it safer for people to use their bicycles to commute to school and to work."

Andy, who rides his bicycle to school every day, told the city council members that the roads should be much safer for bicyclists. He said that bicyclists need more room between the car lanes and the shoulder of the road. He told a frightening story about almost being run off the road by a careless driver.

The city council members agreed with Andy and promised to make some improvements by the upcoming school year.

Begin by introducing a recent event that is important and interesting.

Answer the following in the first paragraph: Who? What? When? Where? Why? How?

Include additional details that give more information about the topic.

End with a concluding sentence.

1. Underline the sentence that introduces the topic of the news article.
2. Circle the words that answer the questions below. If the writer did not answer a question, write, "not answered."

Who? _____   What? _____

Where? _____   When? _____

Why? _____   How? _____

3. Box additional details that the writer uses to give more information about the topic.
4. Which descriptive words does the writer use to describe the event?

_____

_____

Evaluate a News Article

A. Students were asked to write a news article about a recent event in their town. The news article below received a score of 4. When using a 4-point rubric, a score of 4 means "excellent." Read the article and the comments to find out why this article is a success.

Student Model

DRAFT

Bears Take Sunday Stroll
by Marcus

Graceville police reported that residents spotted two black bears walking down the center of Cliff Street on Sunday night around 8 P.M. The bears, believed to be an adult and a cub, were gone when a police officer arrived and have not been sighted since.

Glenda Curtis, owner of Glenda's Café, first spotted the bears as she was closing her café for the evening. "From a distance I thought they were stray dogs sniffing around for food," Mrs. Curtis said. "But as they got closer I knew they were bears. They looked like they were having a grand old time, like a mama bear was taking her cub on a Sunday stroll." Mrs. Curtis was the first to call the police.

Officer Tom Menasha, who reported to the scene, said that recent construction of new homes in the area has taken away some of the black bears' natural habitat. As a result, more black bears have been spotted in recent months. Last month a black bear was seen walking across the football field in Okaloosa Park.

Officer Menasha said that Mrs. Curtis did the right thing by staying inside and calling the police. Black bears might look friendly and even harmless to some, he said, but they have been known to act aggressively at times.

However, Menasha added, the people of Graceville shouldn't worry. The bears, he said probably returned to the woods peacefully.

Great title! It will really grab the reader's attention.

Nice work. You introduce the event with a good lead. You made it strong by using descriptive words.

Good! Your introduction deals with Who? What? When? Where? and Why?

Nice–You use descriptive words to give additional details about the event. Good job!

Nice work—You do not express your personal viewpoint. But you make clear the viewpoints of the different people in the article.

You do a good job of making sure each sentence has a subject and a predicate.

You end the article with a good conclusion.

© Harcourt

Name _____

B. This article received a score of 2. Why did it receive a low score?

Student Model

DRAFT

Salad Days
by Ricky

Do you like salad? Principal Patterson said that the school was planning to build another salad bar in the cafeteria.

The number of students eating salads for lunch is growing. Principal Patterson said that last year only twenty percent of the students ate salad for lunch. This year almost thirty-five percent of the students.

The new salad bar will provide a wider selection of vegetables. It will also give hungry students a choice of soups, such as chicken noodle soup, French onion soup, and lentil soup.

> Good. You use a interrogative sentence as a lead. Use descriptive words to make it stronger.

> You introduce the event in the first paragraph, but you need to include more details to answer the questions *When?* and *Why?*

> This sentence is incomplete. It has a subject but no predicate.

> Good. You give some details about the soups. You could give more details about the vegetables.

C. What score would you give the student's story? Put a number on each line.

	4	3	2	1
Voice _____	☐ The writer uses many descriptive words and sensory details to describe the event.	☐ The writer uses some descriptive words and sensory details to describe the event.	☐ The writer uses few descriptive words and sensory details to describe the event.	☐ The writer uses no descriptive words or sensory details to describe the event.
Word Choice _____	☐ The writer uses a strong lead with descriptive words that sparks the reader's attention.	☐ The writer uses a lead with one or two descriptive words that makes the reader curious.	☐ The writer uses a lead with no descriptive words but makes the reader curious.	☐ The writer does not use a lead to interest the reader.
Conventions _____	☐ The writer uses declarative and interrogative sentences that have a subject and predicate.	☐ The writer uses only declarative sentences, but they all have a subject and predicate.	☐ The writer uses one incomplete declarative or interrogative sentence.	☐ The writer uses more than one incomplete declarative or interrogative sentence.

© Harcourt

Name _____

Extended Writing/Test Prep

On the first two pages of this lesson, you will use what you have learned about voice and word choice to write a longer written work.

A. Read the three choices below. Put a star by the writing activity you would like to do.

1. Respond to a Writing Prompt

Writing Situation: We are all influenced by the people around us, especially by the members of our family.

Directions for Writing: Think about a member of your family that has had a positive influence on your life. Now write an autobiographical narrative about a time that you have spent with this family member. Use descriptive words to describe the family member and to make your feelings and opinions clear to the reader.

2. Choose one of the pieces of writing you started in this unit:

- a character description paragraph (page 10)

- an autobiographical composition (page 16)

- an autobiographical narrative (page 22)

Revise and expand your work into a complete piece of writing. Use what you have learned about voice and word choice.

3. Choose a topic you would like to write about. You may write a character description, an autobiographical composition, or an autobiographical narrative. Use descriptive words to make your writing come alive and to make your viewpoint clear. Also, use a strong lead to draw your reader in.

B. Use the space below and on the next page to plan your writing.

TOPIC: _____

WRITING FORM: _____

HOW WILL I ORGANIZE MY WRITING: _____

_____

© Harcourt

Name _____

C. In the space below, draw a graphic organizer that will help you plan your writing. Fill in the graphic organizer. Write additional notes on the lines below.

Notes

_____

_____

_____

_____

_____

_____

D. Do your writing on another sheet of paper.

Name _____

Answering Multiple-Choice Questions

For questions on pages 34–37, fill in the bubble next to the correct answer.

A. Manuel made the plan below to organize ideas for a paper. Use his plan to answer questions 1–3.

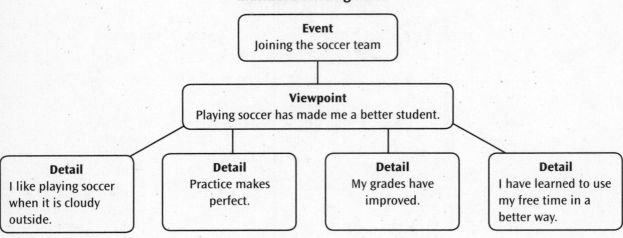

Manuel's Writing Plan

Event
Joining the soccer team

Viewpoint
Playing soccer has made me a better student.

Detail
I like playing soccer when it is cloudy outside.

Detail
Practice makes perfect.

Detail
My grades have improved.

Detail
I have learned to use my free time in a better way.

1. Based on the information in Manuel's Writing Plan, what kind of paper is he planning to write?

   (A) a newspaper story

   (B) a character description paragraph

   (C) an autobiographical composition

   (D) a how-to paragraph

> **Test Tip:**
> A detail makes the viewpoint more clear. Choose the detail that helps explain the writer's feelings or opinions about the topic.

2. Which detail from Manuel's Writing Plan does not make Manuel's viewpoint clearer and should be crossed off the plan?

   (A) I like playing soccer when it is cloudy outside.

   (B) Practice makes perfect.

   (C) My grades have improved.

   (D) I have learned to use my free time in a better way.

3. Based on the information in Manuel's Writing Plan, which detail below makes the viewpoint clearer and should be added to the plan?

   (A) I have made new friends.

   (B) Now I can run a mile under 10 minutes.

   (C) Our soccer jersey has red and yellow stripes.

   (D) I have learned about other countries from reading about soccer.

Name _____

B. The paragraph below is the first draft that Helena wrote. The paragraph contains mistakes. Read the paragraph to answer questions 1–3.

Going Door to Door

(1) I was nervous. (2) I was collecting donations for the school library. (3) My father and I had woken up at sunrise to get an early start. (4) It was the first house of the day. (5) I lightly rapped my knuckles on the door. (6) I listened for a sign of life behind the door, but I heard nothing. (7) I turned to look at my father, who was watching from the sidewalk. (8) I shrugged as if to ask, "How will I collect anything if no one is home?" (9) He made a knocking motion with his hand. (10) I knocked harder this time and turned again to show that no one was home. (11) Suddenly a loud creak startled me. (12) An elderly man was standing at the door. (13) Words tumbled out of my mouth. (14) The next thing I knew, I was holding the first donation of the day!

1. Which sentence below should be added after sentence (1) to provide the reader with more descriptive words?

Ⓐ I get nervous sometimes when I speak with strangers.

Ⓑ There was a frog in my throat and my hand was trembling.

Ⓒ I don't get nervous very often.

Ⓓ I knew I shouldn't have been nervous.

> **Test Tip:**
> Descriptive words, such as sensory details, help the reader picture more vividly what the writer is describing. Choose the sentence that gives you the clearest picture of how the writer was feeling.

2. Which sentence below should be added to the beginning of the paragraph to make a stronger lead?

Ⓐ Who wouldn't think twice about walking up to a stranger's house?

Ⓑ I started with the house on the corner of my street.

Ⓒ The library needed to raise extra money for a new computer.

Ⓓ I walked up the sidewalk toward the house.

3. The writer wants to add the following sentence to the story:

    | I nearly jumped off the porch! |

Where should this be added to provide more vivid details?

Ⓐ after sentence (5)

Ⓑ after sentence (8)

Ⓒ after sentence (9)

Ⓓ after sentence (11)

© Harcourt

Name _____

C. Read the story "Meant for the Water." Choose the word, words, or punctuation mark that best completes questions 1–4.

Meant for the Water

When I was little, my brother Steven used to impress me by swimming across Star Lake and back. ___(1)___ wasn't huge. It wasn't very deep either. Still, I was impressed. Why was I impressed___(2)___ Steven ___(3)___ like an athlete. His arms and legs were long and skinny, and he slouched when he walked. In spite of his appearance, he used to make the round-trip journey effortlessly. On land he seemed awkward, but in the water he was as graceful as a dolphin. The difference was absolutely amazing___(4)___ I think Steven was meant for the water___(5)___

1. Which answer should go in blank (1)?
   - (A) Really
   - (B) The Lake
   - (C) Actually

2. Which answer should go in blank (2)?
   - (A) ?
   - (B) !
   - (C) .

3. Which answer should go in blank (3)?
   - (A) swimming just
   - (B) not appearing
   - (C) didn't look

4. Which answer should go in blank (4)?
   - (A) ?
   - (B) !
   - (C) ,

5. Which answer should go in blank (5)?
   - (A) ?
   - (B) ,
   - (C) .

Test Tips:
Complete sentences have both a subject and a predicate. A subject names whom or what the sentence is about. The predicate tells what the subject is or does.

Choose the word that makes the sentence complete.

© Harcourt

Name _____

D. Read each sentence and pick which type of mistake appears in the underlined section.

1. Kendra's <u>granfather</u> gave her his cherry-brown violin.

   (A) Punctuation error

   (B) Usage error

   (C) Spelling error

2. "<u>Wow? I cant believe that,</u>" Jaime said.

   (A) Usage error

   (B) Punctuation error

   (C) Spelling error

3. The Statue of <u>Liberty are located</u> in New York City.

   (A) Capitalization error

   (B) Spelling error

   (C) Usage error

4. The students <u>lines up</u> after the bell rang.

   (A) Punctuation error

   (B) Usage error

   (C) Capitalization error

5. When is our field trip to <u>the arts museum!</u>

   (A) Spelling error

   (B) Usage error

   (C) Punctuation error

> **Test Tip:**
>
> A declarative sentence makes a statement. It ends with a period.
>
> An interrogative sentence asks a question. It ends with a question mark.
>
> An exclamatory sentence expresses a strong feeling. It ends with an exclamation point.

© Harcourt

Name _____

Identify: Elaborating with Examples

When writers **elaborate with examples,** they go into greater detail about something they have stated in general terms. Examples help the reader fully understand a writer's ideas.

A. Read the following passage, which describes the character Amalia in The *Night of San Juan*. Notice how the writer uses specific examples to illustrate Amalia's personality.

Literature Model

If anyone would have the courage to do that, it was my little sister Amalia. Even though she was only seven, she was also the most daring of the three of us.

We never knew what she would do next. In fact, at that very moment I could see a mischievous grin spreading across her freckled face as two elegant women turned the corner of Calle Sol. Once they strolled down the street in front of us, Amalia swiftly snuck up behind them and flipped their skirts up to expose their lace-trimmed slips.

—from *The Night of San Juan*
by Lulu Delacre

B. Find the general description of Amalia's personality and the examples that help illustrate it for the reader.
   1. Circle the individual words that the writer uses to describe Amalia's character.
   2. Underline the sentences in which the writer uses examples to support this description of Amalia.

C. How do the examples of Amalia's behavior relate to the words the writer has used to describe her? Write your answer below.

_____

_____

_____

_____

© Harcourt

Name _____

Explore: Elaborating with Examples

Elaborating with examples gives readers a more detailed understanding of a general idea. Using plenty of examples also helps tell readers why a general description or statement is an appropriate one.

Elaborate with examples to build support for main ideas.

Elaborate with examples to help readers better understand your ideas.

Elaborate with examples to show your thought process, or reasoning.

Elaborating with examples helps you fully develop your ideas when writing.

A. Read each sentence and think about the idea it presents to the reader. Then write a sentence that uses examples to elaborate on the idea.

Example Although the boy was quite young, he had an impressive vocabulary.

I have heard him use words that even his father had to ask him to explain.

1. The flamingo is the most graceful creature in the animal kingdom.

_____

_____

2. I thought the play was a complete disaster.

_____

_____

3. Of all the students at the music academy, Nicola is the most talented.

_____

_____

B. Here is a sentence from *The Night of San Juan*. What examples in the sentence help to explain why the children are afraid of José Manuel's grandmother? Circle them.

Besides her fear of danger on the street, José Manuel's grandma kept to herself and never smiled, so most of us were afraid of her.

© Harcourt

Name _____

Use: Elaborating with Examples

Before you write a paragraph describing a **personal response**, ask yourself what idea you want to communicate to the reader. Then think about how you can elaborate on your idea with examples. Here is how one student started to think about his response to a book he read.

Example

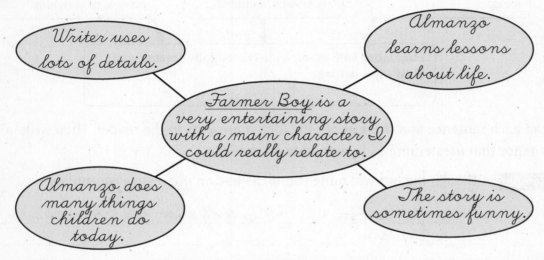

A. Think about a book you have read recently. What did you think of it? Write a topic sentence that describes what you think of the book. Complete the graphic organizer by listing examples that support your statement.

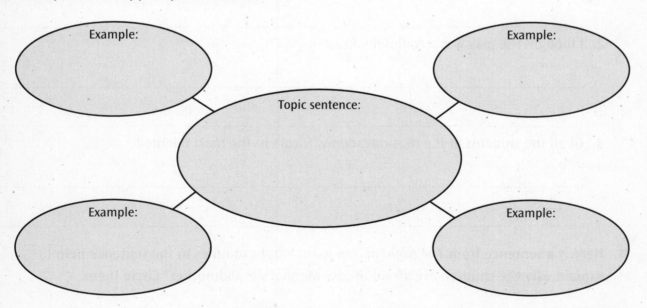

© Harcourt

B. Use the completed graphic organizer to write a paragraph describing your personal response to a book you have read. Write your paragraph on another sheet of paper.

Name _____

The Parts of a Personal Response Paragraph

In a **personal response paragraph,** you give your opinion on a topic and use examples to support your statement. Below is an example of a personal response paragraph written by a fifth-grade student. As you read, think about how the student organized it. Then answer the questions.

Student Model

DRAFT **What a City Boy Thinks of _Farmer Boy_**
by Anthony

> **Introduce** the topic you are writing about.

   Farmer Boy, by Laura Ingalls Wilder, tells the story of Almanzo Wilder, a young boy growing up on a farm in the 1860s. Some people might think that a book set so long ago would not interest today's readers. However, I loved _Farmer Boy_ because it was an entertaining story with a main character I could really relate to. Almanzo does many of the things children do today. Using lots of details, the writer describes Almanzo's life and the important lessons he learns. The story is funny as well as serious. I may live in a big city in the 21st century, but reading about Almanzo's adventures reminded me of my own.

> **State** your opinion.

> **Include** facts, examples, or reasons that support your opinion.

> **Personalize** your response. Tell how the topic relates to your life.

1. Which sentence introduces the topic? Circle it.
2. Which sentence states the writer's opinion? Underline it.
3. Find facts, examples, or reasons that support the writer's opinion of the book. Write two supporting details.

_____

_____

4. How does the writer personalize his response?

_____

_____

Name _____

Evaluate a Personal Response Paragraph

When you evaluate a personal response paragraph, ask yourself whether the writer clearly stated his or her opinion and supported that opinion with plenty of facts, examples, or reasons.

Now use the checklist to evaluate the Student Model. Put a check in the box next to each thing the writer did well. If you do not think the writer did a good job, do not check the box.

- ☐ The topic is introduced.
- ☐ The writer's opinion is clearly stated.
- ☐ There are many specific examples to support the writer's opinion.
- ☐ The writer connects the topic to his or her life.
- ☐ The paragraph is organized in a logical way.

Writer's Grammar
Compound Subjects and Predicates

A compound subject is two or more subjects, joined by a conjunction, that have the same verb. Likewise, a compound predicate has two or more verbs, also joined by a conjunction, that have the same subject.

Compound Subject Joshua and his friend Amina are studying for tomorrow's quiz.

Compound Predicate The performers will sing, dance, or play an instrument.

Rewrite each pair of sentences with a compound subject or compound predicate. Draw a line under each compound subject. Circle each compound predicate.

1. Tanja stole the ball. Tanja kicked the ball. Tanja scored a goal.

_____

2. Xin read *The Friends* over the summer. Xin's sister read *The Friends* over the summer.

_____

3. Carlos will do the dishes after supper. Peter will do the dishes after supper.

_____

4. Harry puts on his glasses. Harry looks closely at the mysterious note.

_____

Name _____

Revise: Adding Examples

One thing the writer could have done better is add more specific examples to support his statements about the book. Here is an example of how the Student Model can be improved.

Example The story is funny as well as serious.

The story is funny as well as serious. When I read how Almanzo fed sticky candy to his pig Lucy, I laughed so hard my stomach hurt!

A. Revise these sentences from the Student Model. Add details and examples. Use the Word Bank to help you.

1. Almanzo does many of the things children do today.

_____

_____

2. Using lots of details, the writer describes Almanzo's life and the important lessons he learns.

_____

_____

Word Bank

chores
importance
honesty
labor
reward
schoolwork
sledding

B. Revise the personal response paragraph you wrote on page 40. Add examples that help to support your opinions. Do your work on a separate sheet of paper.

Name _____

Identify: Staying on Topic

Strong writing **stays on topic**. To stay on topic, writers need to focus on a main idea. They also need to think about their **purpose**, or why they are writing. They need to consider their **audience**, or who will be reading their work, too.

A. Read this passage. Look for the topic, or main idea. Think about what the writer's purpose is and who the audience might be.

Literature Model

When Lung had stepped out of the way, the lion hopped on top of the ball. Then it rolled all around and did tricks. It even scratched itself and tried to bite fleas like a real lion. In the meantime Lung and Ah Sam had been setting up rows of poles. For its finale the lion leaped from one tall pole to another. When the lion hopped down from the ball, Ah Loo and Ah Bing got out of the costume.

They sure were talented folk. I would never have guessed it was two people doing the jumps together.

—from *When the Circus Came to Town*
by Laurence Yep

B. Identify the writer's topic.

1. Draw a box around the topic sentence. Hint: It is neither the first nor the last sentence.
2. Underline the words or phrases that show the writer's focus on this main idea.

C. What do you think is the author's purpose in writing this passage? For whom do you think he is writing?

_____

_____

_____

_____

© Harcourt

Name _____

Explore: Staying on Topic

To keep a reader's interest, focus your writing. Stay on topic and develop your main idea fully. Think about why you are writing and who will read your writing. Knowing your purpose and audience will help you decide how to write about your topic.

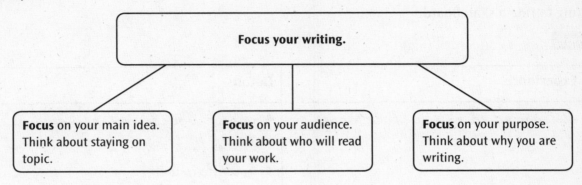

A. Read each sentence and think about the reason for writing it. Then circle the word that best describes the writer's purpose.

Example   On average, people visit shopping centers five times a month.

persuade   describe   (inform)   entertain

1. The train station smelled warm and brown, like hay in a sunny barn.

persuade   describe   inform   entertain

2. Once upon a time, in a kingdom far, far away, there was a girl who played a golden flute.

persuade   describe   inform   entertain

3. This fantastic dance troupe will be in town for one week only, so buy tickets soon! You'll be sorry if you miss it.

persuade   describe   inform   entertain

B. Read this paragraph from *When the Circus Came to Town*. Think about what main idea the writer is developing. Then write a topic sentence for the paragraph.

As Ah Sam handed her the benches, Ah Loo began to build a pyramid of benches on top of Ah Bing's feet and climb up it. Higher and higher went the pyramid. Higher and higher went Ah Loo. Finally she was as high as the tallest building. Everyone had to lean far back to look up at her as she twirled and spun, graceful as a spider on a thread.

_____

_____

© Harcourt

Name _____

Use: Staying on Topic

One purpose for writing a **journal entry** is to remember an experience or event. The audience for a journal entry is yourself, although you may share the entry with others. Before you write a journal entry, list details that you will use to focus your chosen topic. Here is how one student started to record details about learning to ride a skateboard.

Example

Experience	Details
I learned to ride a skateboard.	• purple board with red and black flames • birthday wish • I was nervous but determined.

A. Think about a time you learned to do something new. In the left column, write a sentence that states what you learned. In the right column, list details that will help you stay on topic when you write.

Experience	Details

B. Use the details from your chart to write a journal entry describing a time you learned to do something new. Write your entry on another sheet of paper.

© Harcourt

Name _____

The Parts of a Journal Entry

A **journal entry** is a daily record of observations written in first person, using words such as *I, me,* and *mine.* An entry may include both observations about events and personal thoughts or feelings. Below is an example of a journal entry written by a fifth-grade student. As you read, think about how the student organized it. Then answer the questions.

Student Model

DRAFT

Learning to Ride
by Evangeline

Monday, September 20

I've had my skateboard for two years. It's a beautiful purple board with red and black flames. I've wanted to learn to ride it for as long as I've had it, but after all this time I still haven't learned.

Yesterday all of that changed. Saturday was my 10th birthday. As I woke up I wished, "Let me finally learn to ride my skateboard!" Early the next day I went outside. I was nervous, but determined.

My first few tries were disastrous. I fell each time. Then my sister came outside. She is really good at basketball. She kept encouraging me, saying, "You can do it, Evangeline." And suddenly, I could! I was so happy, I rode up and down the street all day.

Date the entry at the top of the page.

Introduce your topic. Set the stage for the event you will describe.

Describe events in order.

Use simple and compound subjects, predicates, and sentences.

Develop your topic by adding relevant details that bring the description to life for the reader.

Include feelings as well as observations.

1. Which sentences introduce the topic? Circle them.
2. Which sentence seems to be off topic? Underline it.
3. Find details that bring the event to life. Write three details on the line below.

_____

_____

4. Which words show the writer's feelings?

_____

_____

Name _____

Evaluate a Journal Entry

When you evaluate a journal entry, ask yourself whether the writer stays focused
on a specific topic. You should also consider whether the writing clearly shows
the writer's purpose and intended audience.

Now use the checklist to evaluate the Student Model. Put a check in the box
next to each thing the writer did well. If you do not think the writer did a good
job, do not check the box.

☐ The entry is focused on a specific topic.
☐ The entry is written in first person and shows the writer's feelings.
☐ Events are described in order.
☐ The writer uses specific and relevant details to develop the topic.
☐ The writer uses simple and compound subjects, predicates, and sentences.

Writer's Grammar
Simple and Compound Sentences

A **simple sentence** is a group of words that together express one complete
thought. It includes a simple or compound subject and a simple or
compound predicate. A **compound sentence** is made up of two or more
simples sentences joined by conjunctions, such as *and, but,* or *or.*

Simple Sentences
Danita and her friends go to the park after school.
The performers jumped and twirled around the stage.

Compound Sentences
You can go to the movies, or you can go swimming.
Sometimes I make pancakes for breakfast, but today I made waffles.

Label each sentence *simple* or *compound*.

1. I like to ride my bike, and my sister likes to go hiking. _____

2. The crowd shouted and applauded as the home team took the lead. _____

3. My cousin Tal and I went to the market to buy apples and carrots. _____

5. Father put his glasses on the table, or he left them in the car. _____

6. Insects have three basic body parts: the head, thorax, and abdomen. _____

7. Some people say that nuclear power is a cheap source of energy, but others are concerned
about its danger. _____

Name _____

Revise: Adding Relevant Details

One thing the writer could have done better is to add specific and relevant details to make her journal entry really come alive. Here is an example of how the Student Model can be improved.

Example I've wanted to learn to ride it for as long as I've had it, but after all this time I still haven't learned.

I've wanted to learn to ride it for as long as I've had it, but after all this time the only skill I have is in getting bruises.

A. Revise these sentences. Add relevant details. Use the Word Bank to help you.

1. Early the next day I went outside.

_____

_____

_____

2. I fell each time.

_____

_____

3. She is really good at basketball.

_____

_____

Word Bank
bravely
champion
elbow pads
helmet
pavement
smashed
supportive

B. Revise the journal entry you wrote on page 46. Focus your writing by adding relevant details and removing details that stray from your topic. Do your work on a separate sheet of paper.

_____

_____

_____

© Harcourt

Name _____

Identify: Time-Order Words

Time-order words include words and phrases such as *finally, at that time,* and *next*. These transition words help readers understand the sequence in which events happen.

A. Read the following passage from *When Washington Crossed the Delaware*. Look for words that indicate the sequence of events.

Literature Model

About one o'clock in the morning on January 3, Washington and the main body of his army moved out. Cannon wheels were muffled with rags. Officers whispered orders. The Americans did everything they could to be quiet, and their plan worked. It was dawn before Cornwallis realized they were gone.

The morning was clear and cold as Washington and his men neared Princeton. In farmland outside the town a part of the American army encountered British troops. During the fight that followed, many of the Americans fell. The dazed survivors retreated.

—from *When Washington Crossed the Delaware*
by Lynne Cheney

B. Identify the words that tell the sequence of events in the passage.
1. Underline the phrase that tells you the time of the event in the first sentence.
2. Circle the words that tell you when Cornwallis realized the army was gone.
3. Draw a box around the words that tell you when Washington and his men arrived in Princeton.
4. Write the phrase that tells you what happened after the American army encountered the British. Double underline the two time-order words in that phrase.

_____

C. About how much time passes from the beginning of the passage to the end? How do you know?

_____

_____

_____

_____

Name _____

Explore: Time-Order Words

Use time-order words to organize the sequence of events in your writing. Words that tell sequence also help readers make the transition from one paragraph to the next, or one sentence to the next.

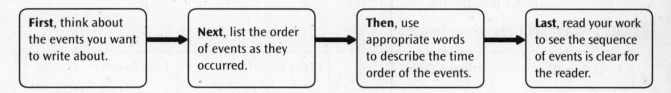

| First, think about the events you want to write about. | → | Next, list the order of events as they occurred. | → | Then, use appropriate words to describe the time order of the events. | → | Last, read your work to see the sequence of events is clear for the reader. |

A. Read each sentence. Then circle the word or words that indicate sequence, or time order.

Example (After) brushing her teeth and washing her face, Claudia was ready for bed.

1. Bao wasn't sure he liked his new school, but he soon found friends.

2. At that very moment, rain began to pour from the sky.

3. When Yuri found out he had won airplane tickets, he packed his bags immediately.

B. Read these sentences from *When Washington Crossed the Delaware*. Fill in the blanks with transition words to make the sequence of events clear. Use the Word Bank to help you.

The rest of the Hessians retreated, but the Americans _____ had them surrounded…. _____ from the time it had started, the Battle of Trenton was over. With few losses of their own the Americans had captured nearly nine hundred Hessians. _____ many defeats they had won a great victory.

Word Bank
after
soon
two hours

C. Now rewrite the sentences. Use different words to show the sequence of events. Be careful not to change the order of events. Do your writing on another sheet of paper.

_____

_____

© Harcourt

Name _____

Use: Time-Order Words

A **biography** is an account of someone's life. Before you write a biography, list some of the important events in that person's life. One way to order the events is in chronological, or time, order. Here is how one student started to plan to write about the events in her great-grandmother's life.

Example Who: My Great-Grandmother

First Event:	Next Event:	Next Event:	Last Event:
Ishvani Kumar was born in 1915.	left India at age 16 and moved to Paris, France	moved to New York City in 1941 to study art	met Hamilton Sanders at artist's studio and they began working together

A. Think about a person you know who would make a good subject for a biography. It can be a friend, a family member, or someone you know about. Write that person's name on the line. Then complete the graphic organizer with the most important events in that person's life. Be sure to put the events in chronological order.

Who:

First Event:	Next Event:	Next Event:	Last Event:

B. Use the information from your graphic organizer to draft a biographical sketch of a person you would like to write about. Write your biography on another sheet of paper.

Name _____

The Parts of a Biography

A **biography** is a factual narrative about an individual life. It may be told in a book, a movie, or other form of media. Here is an example of a biographical sketch written by a fifth-grade student. As you read, think about how the student organized it. Then answer the questions.

Student Model

DRAFT

Ishvani Kumar
by Sunita

My great-grandmother, Ishvani Kumar, was born in Bombay, India, in 1915. When she was just 16, she left India to escape a marriage she did not want. She soon started taking sculpting classes. One day, while walking through the great halls of the Louvre, she decided art was her life's passion. She moved to Paris, France, a city she described as "fascinating."

In 1939, Ishvani moved to New York City to continue studying art. She felt uncertain of whether she liked this new city. During her first year, she met many other artists, as well as writers and performers. Then in January of 1943, she met a painter named Hamilton Sanders at the studio of an artist friend. They immediately began what would become a lifetime of collaboration.

> **Introduce** the subject and tell how you are related to or know about that person.

> **Organize** your sketch. Describe each event in appropriate time-order sequence.

> **Include** time-order words to help readers follow from one event to another.

> **Use prepositional phrases** to vary your sentences.

1. Which sentence introduces the subject of the biography? Underline it.
2. Circle the transition words or phrases that help readers follow the sequence of events.
3. Write other words or phrases that the writer uses to make clear the sequence of events for the reader.

_____

4. How old was Ishvani Kumar when she met Hamilton Sanders? How do you know?

_____

_____

_____

_____

Name _____

Evaluate a Biography

When you evaluate a biography, think about whether the writer used a clear sequence of events to tell readers about the subject's life. You should also look for transition words and phrases that help show the time order of events.

Now use the checklist to evaluate the Student Model. Put a check in the box next to each thing the writer did well. If you do not think the writer did a good job, do not check the box.

☐ The writer introduces the subject and identifies the writer-subject relationship.
☐ The life events that are described are organized in a clear and appropriate time-order sequence.
☐ The writer includes transitional time-order words to help readers follow the sequence of events.
☐ The writer varies the sentences by using prepositional phrases.

Writer's Grammar
Prepositional Phrases

A **prepositional phrase** begins with a preposition and includes an object of the preposition. For example, in the sentence *The moon was covered by a thin purple cloud,* the noun *cloud* is the object of the preposition *by*. Common prepositions include the words *by, of, about, to, through, from, between, after, when,* and *in*.

Some prepositional phrases modify, or describe, nouns or pronouns. These prepositional phrases are called **adjective phrases**. They tell *what kind* or *which one*.

Example A book that someone writes about another person's life is called a *biography*.

Other prepositional phrases modify verbs or adverbs. These prepositional phrases are called **adverb phrases**. They tell *when, where, how,* or *why*.

Example In a few days, we will forget this ever happened.

Read each sentence. Then underline each preposition and circle its object. Some sentences may have more than one prepositional phrase.

1. In my school library, I saw the stories of Rudyard Kipling.

2. The children played in the woods for the whole afternoon.

3. Thank Aunt Sarah for the present she brought for you.

4. The desk at the front of the room was covered with books.

© Harcourt

Name _____

Revise: Putting Events in Time Order

One thing the writer of the biographical sketch could have done better is to organize events in clear chronological order. Here is how the first paragraph of the sketch could be improved.

Example   My great-grandmother, Ishvani Kumar, was born in Bombay, India, in 1915. When she was just 16, she left India to escape a marriage she did not want. She soon started taking sculpting classes. One day, while walking through the great halls of the Louvre, she decided that art was her life's passion. She moved to Paris, France, a city she described as "fascinating."

My great-grandmother, Ishvani Kumar, was born in Bombay, India in 1915. When she was just 16, she left India to escape a marriage she did not want. She moved to Paris, France, a city she described as "fascinating." One day, while walking through the great halls of the Louvre, she decided that art was her life's passion. She started taking sculpting classes soon after.

A. Revise this paragraph. Put events in appropriate time order. Use transition words from the Word Bank to help you.

Word Bank

after
immediately
then

1.   She pays the cashier for her new brushes, colored paints, and canvas. She sprints into the art store and goes to the painting section. Her mom parks the car. Josephine jumps out the car in a flash.

_____

_____

_____

_____

B. Revise the biography you wrote on page 52. Check that all events are in time order and that there are transition words to help the reader follow the sequence of events. Write your revision on another sheet of paper.

Name _____

Review Writer's Craft

Effective writers produce focused writing. Writing that is focused stays on topic and elaborates with plenty of examples. Good writers also use time-order words to help readers make the transition from one idea, or action, to the next.

A. Read the passage below. Notice how the writer stays on topic and uses examples to elaborate on the ideas. Also notice how the writer uses transition words to help readers follow the sequence of events.

Literature Model

The horse would always be Charlie's dream, but as soon as Nina went to work, he had to become her horse, too. She had studied in Italy for eleven years. Her favorite Renaissance artist was Verrochio, Leonardo's teacher. It was lucky that she was there to carry on with Charlie's dream.

First Nina made an eight-foot clay horse. From it a second eight-foot horse was made of plaster. Using the plaster model as a guide, a twenty-four-foot horse was made in clay.

Everyone went to work to get the horse exactly right. Finally he was ready to be cast in bronze.

—from *Leonardo's Horse*
by Jean Fritz

B. Review why the writing in this passage is effective.

1. Underline the topic sentence. Look for the sentence that establishes the writer's main idea.
2. Draw a box around the words that show time order.
3. The writer believes it was lucky that Nina was there to help realize Charlie's dream. List the examples that she gives to support this idea.

_____

_____

C. What do you think is the purpose of describing Nina's work process?

_____

_____

Name _____

Review Writer's Craft

Elaborating with examples and staying on topic helps writers present their ideas. Using time-order words keeps writing organized and helps readers follow the sequence of events.

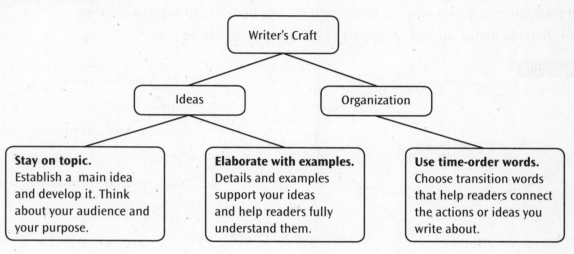

A. Read this paragraph from *Leonardo's Horse*.

> But how could such a large bronze sculpture stand on two legs? First they built a steel skeleton inside the body of the horse to support the sides, and then they inserted steel tubes in the two legs. The tubes were bolted to steel anchor plates below the hooves and embedded in concrete.

B. Match each piece of text from the paragraph to the kind of effective writing it represents.

Example

_____ The tubes were bolted to steel anchor plates below the hooves and embedded in concrete.

_____ But how could such a large bronze sculpture stand on two legs?

_____ First they built a steel…

A. topic question that establishes the main idea

B. time-order words that organize the sequence of events

C. detail that supports the main idea

C. Write another detail that you could add to the paragraph.

_____

_____

_____

Review Writer's Craft

When you write a **summary**, you retell the most important information of a selection in your own words. Before you write a summary, you need to think about your purpose and audience. You also need to think about how to organize the information so it makes sense to readers. Here is how one fifth-grade student began thinking about summarizing part of a magazine article he read.

Example

first, waits for prey

when prey comes it senses vibrations and uses its tongue to smell the animal

Main Idea
how rattlesnakes find and eat prey,

after venom stuns prey, it swallows it whole

when it finally knows where prey is, it strikes

A. Use the chart above to answer the questions below.

1. How has the student organized the information from the article?

_____

_____

2. Use the information listed in the web. Write a topic sentence for the summary.

_____

_____

3. What time-order words has the student listed to help tell a sequence of events?

_____

© Harcourt

Name _____

The Parts of a Summary

A short statement of the most important ideas in a passage or text is called a **summary.** A summary should be written in a writer's own words. Below is an example of a summary written by a fifth-grade student. As you read, think about how the student organized it. Then answer the questions.

Student Model

DRAFT

How a Rattlesnake Eats
by Neal

Rattlesnakes are very clever predators. To find prey, they first find a place where animals are likely to be and wait. This is probably pretty boring for the snake. When an animal comes near, the rattlesnake knows because it feels the vibrations in the ground and smells the animal's scent with its tongue. Then it uses heat-sensitive pits in its face to sense the body heat coming from the prey. Finally, when the snake knows exactly where the animal is, it strikes. Venom from the snakebite stuns the animal. After striking, the snake draws back from the animal and waits for it to become paralyzed. Then it swallows the animal whole. Some rattlesnakes actually eat lizards.

> **Introduce** the topic of the summary by stating the main idea of the passage.

> **Organize** ideas in the order they were presented in the selection. **Use transitions** to connect ideas or show the sequence of events.

> **Develop** your summary by including only the most important ideas. Do not mention minor details or your own ideas or opinions.

1. What is the writer's purpose in this paragraph?

_____

_____

2. Which sentence introduces the topic of the summary? Underline it.

3. What transition or time-order words does the writer use? Circle them.

4. Which two sentences could be left out of the summary? Draw a box around them. Explain why they should be left out.

_____

_____

_____

_____

Name _____

Evaluate a Summary

A. Two students were asked to write a summary of an article they read recently. The summary below got a score of 4. When using a 4-point rubric, a score of 4 means "excellent." Read the summary and teacher comments. Find out why this summary is a success.

Student Model

Protecting the California Condor
by Nancy

Twenty-five years after starting a captive-breeding program, scientists and other conservationists continue their work to protect the endangered population of California condors. The California condor was first listed as an endangered species in 1967, when the population was estimated to be about 60 birds. By 1982, there were less than 30 California condors left in the wild. At that time, the San Diego Zoo and the Los Angeles Zoo got together with government organizations to begin a program to help the population grow. First, the birds were captured and placed in special facilities. Then scientists began a breeding program that included raising chicks with condor puppets. Ten years later, the first condors born in captivity were released. With more work, the population of birds grew to 200. Today, there are about 290 California condors. About 140 of those live in the wild.

> Good! You introduced your summary by stating the main idea of the article.

> You've done a good job organizing ideas and events. That's important.

> You've done an excellent job using time-order words. The reader can easily follow the sequence of events.

> You really kept your focus. Your summary includes the most important ideas and doesn't include any unnecessary ones. Great job!

© Harcourt

Name _____

B. This summary got a score of 2. Why did it get a low score?

Student Model

Dance of the Honeybees
by Jana

Honeybees communicate by dancing and they also produce honey. I really like to eat peanut butter and honey sandwiches. Sometimes honeybees dance quickly and sometimes they dance slowly. They dance to tell each other where to find food. Food is nectar, the sweet juice of a flower. They might run in a circle or move in a figure eight. Different dances are used to communicate how far away the food is from the hive. The other bees follow the dance and the smell of the nectar on the dancing bee. Then they go in search of the food source.

State your topic clearly in your first sentence. What is the main idea of the selection you read?

This detail is off topic. Don't introduce your own opinions in a summary.

Is the sequence of ideas clear? You have some good supporting information here, but you need to place related ideas next to each other and use more transitions.

C. What score would you give the student's summary? Put a number on each line.

	4	3	2	1
Focus/Ideas _____	☐ The summary is very focused. The main idea is clearly stated.	☐ The summary is generally focused. The main idea is stated.	☐ The summary is somewhat focused. The main idea is not stated clearly.	☐ The summary lacks focus. The main idea of the selection is not stated.
Organization _____	☐ The ideas progress in a logical way. There are transition words to make the relationship among ideas clear.	☐ The organization is mostly clear. Some transitions are used.	☐ The summary shifts from one topic to another. Ideas are out of order. There are few or no transitions.	☐ The summary has little or no sense of organization.
Conventions _____	☐ The writer uses a number of simple and compound subjects, predicates, and sentences, and uses several prepositional phrases.	☐ The writer uses some simple and compound subjects, predicates, and sentences, and uses some prepositional phrases.	☐ The writer uses a few simple and compound subjects, predicates, and sentences, and uses a few prepositional phrases.	☐ The writer uses no simple and compound subjects, predicates, and sentences, and uses no prepositional phrases.

© Harcourt

Name _____

Extended Writing/Test Prep

On the first two pages of this lesson, you will use what you have learned about ideas and organization to write a longer written work.

A. Read the three choices below. Put a star by the writing activity you would like to do.

1. Respond to a Writing Prompt

Writing Situation: Think about a time something exciting happened. Why do you remember this event?

Directions for Writing: Think about what details are relevant to your retelling of an exciting event. Now, write a journal entry retelling what you saw, thought, and felt. Use time-order words to help retell the events.

2. Choose one of the pieces of writing you started in this unit:

- a personal response paragraph (page 40)

- a journal entry (page 46)

- a biography (page 52)

Revise and expand your work into a complete piece of writing. Use what you have learned about ideas and organization.

3. Choose a topic you would like to write about. Read an article written about this topic, then write a summary of the article. Include the most important ideas in your summary.

B. Use the space below and on the next page to plan your writing.

TOPIC: _____

WRITING FORM: _____

HOW WILL I ORGANIZE MY WRITING: _____

_____

_____

_____

© Harcourt

Name _____

C. In the space below, draw a graphic organizer that will help you plan your writing. Fill in the graphic organizer. Write additional notes on the lines below.

Notes

_____

_____

_____

_____

_____

_____

_____

D. Do your writing on another sheet of paper.

Answering Multiple-Choice Questions

For questions on pages 64–67, fill in the bubble next to the correct answer.

A. Ellen made the plan below to organize ideas for a paper. Use her plan to answer questions 1–3.

Ellen's Writing Plan

Example:
It includes Irish culture and tells about a local legend.

Example:
It is set in a beautiful fishing village in western Ireland.

Topic Sentence:
I think "The Secret of Roan Inish" is a fantastic movie for several reasons.

Example:
The main character in the movie is a girl my age.

Example:
I once went fishing with my cousins.

1. Which example from Ellen's Writing Plan does not support the topic sentence and should be taken off the plan?

   (A) It includes Irish culture and tells about a local legend.
   (B) It is set in a beautiful fishing village in western Ireland.
   (C) I once went fishing with my cousins.
   (D) The main character in the movie is a girl my age.

> **Test Tip:**
> Read all the parts of Ellen's Writing Plan before you answer the questions.

2. Based on the information in Ellen's Writing Plan, which example below is on topic and should be added to the plan?

   (A) The movie tells a simple and charming story.
   (B) I watch a lot of movies.
   (C) Storytelling is a special skill.
   (D) Catching fish can be very hard work.

3. Based on the information in Ellen's Writing Plan, what kind of paper is Ellen planning to write?

   (A) a paper that compares two movies Ellen saw
   (B) a report that gives facts about western Ireland
   (C) a paper that tells about Ellen's visit to Ireland
   (D) a paper that explains Ellen's response to a movie

Name _____

B. Max wrote the following journal entry. The entry contains mistakes. Read the journal entry to answer questions 1–3.

Saturday, October 5

(1) I got my dog Lolly about six months ago. (2) She now weighs 15 pounds and is golden brown with a snowy white streak on her forehead. (3) Her eyes are brown, and they are always smiling. (4) My cat Lucy has green eyes.

(5) My brother and I have been trying to teach Lolly tricks for the past three months. (6) But after hours and hours of training, she still did not understand any of our commands.

(7) Today was different. (8) Lolly followed every single command we gave her. (9) I can't believe it! (10) Now I'm thinking about entering her in the local dog show.

1. Which sentence is off topic and should be taken out of the entry?
   - Ⓐ sentence (1)
   - Ⓑ sentence (4)
   - Ⓒ sentence (6)
   - Ⓓ sentence (10)

> **Test Tip:**
> Staying on topic means focusing on a main idea. It also means thinking about the purpose and audience.

2. Which sentence below should be added after sentence (6) to support the ideas in the second paragraph?
   - Ⓐ She would sit when we asked her to lie down and lie down when we asked her to fetch.
   - Ⓑ I feed Lolly twice a day, and I walk her three times a day.
   - Ⓒ My brother can get her to sit up and beg, if he offers her a treat.
   - Ⓓ Lolly was adopted from the animal shelter on Smith Street.

3. The writer wants to add the following sentence to the story:

   | Now she sits, lies down, rolls over, and fetches. |

   Where would this detail be added to correctly organize the ideas?
   - Ⓐ after sentence (2)
   - Ⓑ after sentence (5)
   - Ⓒ after sentence (8)
   - Ⓓ after sentence (10)

Name _____

C. Read the paragraph, "Into the Ice." Choose the word or words that correctly completes questions 1–5.

Into the Ice

In December of 1914, Ernest Shackleton and a crew of about twenty-five men left England for Antarctica. ___(1)___ its way, the ship entered a pack of ice in the ocean. Shackleton patiently waited for an opening in the ice. ___(2)___ several days passed, Shackleton ___(3)___ his crew realized they were stuck. ___(4)___, the men continued to use the ship as a shelter from the wind and bitter cold. Finally, the pressure of the ice threatened to snap the ship into pieces. The ship was completely destroyed, ___(5)___ the crew unloaded all of the food, equipment, and supplies. They would make camp on the ice.

1. Which answer should go in blank (1)?
   - Ⓐ After
   - Ⓑ On
   - Ⓒ By

2. Which answer should go in blank (2)?
   - Ⓐ After
   - Ⓑ Immediately
   - Ⓒ Meanwhile

3. Which answer should go in blank (3)?
   - Ⓐ but
   - Ⓑ or
   - Ⓒ and

> **Test Tip:**
> Prepositional phrases tell *what kind, which one, when, where, how,* or *why.*

4. Which answer should go in blank (4)?
   - Ⓐ For months
   - Ⓑ Over the mountain
   - Ⓒ Because

5. Which answer should go in blank (5)?
   - Ⓐ because
   - Ⓑ so
   - Ⓒ or

© Harcourt

Name _____

D. Read and answer questions 1–3.

1. Combine the sentences in the box to make one sentence.

> Fiona ate orange slices.
> Sam ate strawberries.

Which sentence below correctly combines the sentences in the box?

(A)   Fiona ate orange slices, but Sam ate strawberries.

(B)   Fiona and Sam ate orange slices and strawberries.

(C)   Fiona ate orange slices and strawberries.

2. Combine the sentences in the box to make one sentence.

> Leo took a walk.
> Leo went to the park.
> Leo played basketball with her friends.

Which sentence below correctly combines the sentences in the box?

(A)   Leo took a walk to the park, and Leo played basketball.

(B)   Leo walked in the park, and went to play basketball with her friends.

(C)   Leo took a walk, went to the park, and played basketball with his friends.

3. Combine the sentences in the box to make one sentence.

> Aunt Sal will take us swimming.
> Uncle Terry will take us swimming.

Which sentence below correctly combines the sentences in the box?

(A)   Aunt Sal takes Uncle Terry swimming.

(B)   Aunt Sal or Uncle Terry will take us swimming.

(C)   We go swimming with Aunt Sal and Uncle Terry.

Test Tip:

Combine two subjects with the same verb to make a compound subject.

Combine two verbs with the same subject to make a compound predicate.

Compound subjects and predicates are joined with conjunctions such as *and* and *or*.

Compound sentences are two simple sentences joined with conjunctions such as *and, but, so,* and *or*.

© Harcourt

Name _____

Identify: Sentence Beginnings

One way to make your writing more effective is to begin your sentences in
different ways. Most sentences start with a subject followed by a predicate. They
can also start with a single word, such as *Immediately*, or with a prepositional
phrase such as *Once every six thousand years*. There are other ways, too. Changing
the way you start your sentences can make your writing more interesting.

A. Read the following passage from *Sailing Home: A Story of a Childhood at Sea*.
Notice how the writer uses different sentence beginnings to describe the hours
after a big storm.

Literature Model

Gradually, the storm ended, and the sea became calm.

"Time to get our celebration ready," said Father. He had never sounded so happy.

With all of us helping, everything was soon put back where it belonged.

"Girls, hang all this ribbon and tinsel up everywhere. And Albert, you're in charge
of decorating the wooden Christmas tree, the one the carpenter made for us."
Mother was excited.

"Don't look, I'm about to bring out the presents. Your father has a surprise for you,
too, don't you, dear?"

We all laughed because we knew what Father's surprise always was at Christmas.
He became Santa.

—from *Sailing Home: A Story of a Childhood at Sea*
by Gloria Rand

B. Identify the examples of different sentence beginnings in the passage.
1. Underline the sentence that begins with a single introductory word that tells *how*.
2. Draw a box around a sentence that begins with a prepositional phrase that tells *who*.
3. Circle a sentence that begins with a command.

C. How do the sentences in this passage sound and look different from each other?

_____

_____

Name _____

Explore: Sentence Beginnings

The most basic sentence style is a subject followed by a predicate. But following this pattern all of the time can make your writing dull. To introduce variety into your sentences, try beginning them with single words, phrases, or clauses.

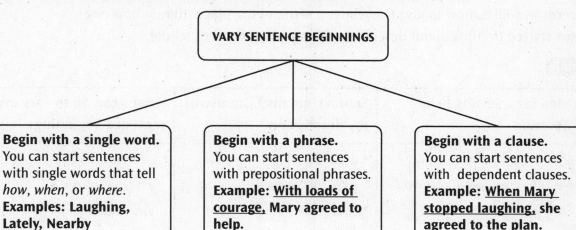

VARY SENTENCE BEGINNINGS

Begin with a single word. You can start sentences with single words that tell *how*, *when*, or *where*. **Examples: Laughing, Lately, Nearby**

Begin with a phrase. You can start sentences with prepositional phrases. **Example: With loads of courage, Mary agreed to help.**

Begin with a clause. You can start sentences with dependent clauses. **Example: When Mary stopped laughing, she agreed to the plan.**

A. Write a new sentence that begins in a different way. To change the beginning, you may rearrange the words from the original sentence. You may also add single words, phrases, or clauses to introduce variety.

> **Example** Original Sentence: The rescue workers quickly raced to the scene.
>
> New Sentence: _Quickly, the rescue workers raced to the scene._

1. Rosa picked many pretty flowers in the field.

_____

2. Derek expressed his frustration by yelling loudly across the field.

_____

B. Read the following sentence *from Sailing Home: A Story of a Childhood at Sea*.

> We had just started to put up the red and green garlands and ropes of sparkling tinsel when father rushed in.

C. Rewrite the sentence in Part B. Begin the sentence in a different way, but be careful not to change its meaning.

_____

_____

© Harcourt

Writer's Companion • UNIT 3
Lesson 11 *Sentence Beginnings*

Name _____

Use: Sentence Beginnings

A good **descriptive paragraph** allows a reader to see, hear, smell, touch, and
sometimes even taste what is being described. Before you write a paragraph
that describes a setting, think about how you can vary the beginnings of your
sentences as well as how to give the reader a sense of the place. Here is how one
student started to think about describing an empty lot near her school.

Example

Idea for a setting I can describe	Sensory details I can use in my description	What I can do to vary my sentence beginnings
the empty lot I see on the way to school each day	• silver color of the chain fence • whirring of machinery in lot next door • smell of trash and flowers	• start with prepositional phrases • start with a single word that tells when or how

A. Think about a place you see every day. What is unique about this setting? Think about
how you can help your readers understand the place's atmosphere, or mood. Then
complete the chart.

Idea for a setting I can describe	Sensory details I can use in my description	What I can do to vary my sentence beginnings

B. Use your completed chart to draft a paragraph describing a place you see every day. Write
your paragraph on another sheet of paper.

Name _____

The Parts of a Descriptive Paragraph

An effective **descriptive paragraph** about a setting should give the reader a clear sense of what the place is like. Good writers do not just tell where a place is, they elaborate with details that show how the place looks, sounds, smells, or feels. Below is an example of a descriptive paragraph written by a fifth-grade student. As you read it, think about how the student organized it. Then answer the questions.

Student Model

The Empty Lot
by Darla

The empty lot is surrounded by silver metal fencing on all four sides. Noisy whirring from the machine shop next door pounds in my head as I stop to look at the vacant space. The smell of trash occasionally blends with the scent of the purple flowers growing on the chain fence. I turn to look with distaste at the plastic bag blowing in a far corner. When the wind stops blowing, the bag settles on the ground. I am late for school. I drop my hand from the sticky fence, and I turn to leave.

> **Introduce** the place you are writing about.

> **Organize** your ideas so that your writing flows in a logical way.

> **Develop** an image for readers by using details that appeal to the senses.

1. Which sentence introduces the place being described? Underline it.
2. Which sentence does not belong in the description? Circle it.
3. Find details that appeal to the senses of sight, sound, smell, and touch. Write an example of each.

   sight: _____   smell: _____

   sound: _____   touch: _____

4. What do the sensory details tell you about the empty lot?

   _____

   _____

© Harcourt

Name _____

Evaluate a Descriptive Paragraph

When you evaluate a descriptive paragraph of a setting, ask yourself how well you were able to picture the place the writer described.

Now use the checklist to evaluate the Student Model. Put a check in the box next to each thing the writer did well. If you do not think the writer did a good job, do not check the box.

- ☐ The writer introduced the place being described.
- ☐ The ideas flow clearly in an order that makes sense.
- ☐ There are many details that appeal to the senses.
- ☐ The writer used different sentence beginnings.

Writer's Grammar
Common and Proper Nouns

A *common noun* is a general name for a person, place, or thing. Common nouns are not capitalized unless they begin a sentence, are part of a title, or begin a quotation. A *proper noun* names a particular person, place, or thing. Proper nouns are capitalized. Here are some examples:

Example **Common Nouns:** architect, holiday, building, state

Proper Nouns: Maya Lin, Memorial Day, Chrysler Building, Hawaii

Rewrite each sentence. Correct any errors in capitalization.

1. I know uncle Steve lives in California, but he is originally from mexico.

_____

_____

2. Antonia and I went to a Los Angeles Lakers Game last saturday.

_____

_____

3. Have you seen the Martin Luther King, jr. National historic site in Atlanta, ga?

_____

© Harcourt

Name _____

Revise: Changing Word Order

One thing the writer might have done better is to start her sentences in different ways. Here is an example of how the writer might have changed the order of her words in the Student Model.

Example **Original:** The empty lot is surrounded by silver metal fencing on all four sides.

Revision: _Silver metal fencing surrounds the empty lot on all four sides._

A. **Revise these sentences. Change word order and add words or phrases.**

1. The smell of trash occasionally blends with the scent of the purple flowers growing on the chain fence.

_____

_____

2. I turn to look with distaste at the plastic bag blowing in a far corner.

_____

_____

3. I drop my hand from the sticky fence, and I turn to leave.

_____

_____

B. **Revise the draft you wrote on page 70. Change word order to add variety to your sentence beginnings. Use another sheet of paper if necessary.**

_____

_____

_____

_____

_____

_____

Name _____

Identify: Making Clear Comparisons and Contrasts

When you **compare,** you focus on likenesses. When you **contrast**, you examine differences. Writing that compares and contrasts look at how the people, objects, places, or events in the text are alike and different.

A. Read this passage from *Ultimate Field Trip 3: Wading into Marine Biology*. Notice how the writer suggests similarities and differences in the animals she describes.

Literature Model

This is the tidal zone—land covered and uncovered by the ocean as the tide climbs up and down the shore. To survive, the plants and animals of the tidal zone must be able to adjust to many different conditions. Snails creep along, for example, until the waves roll in. Then they attach themselves to rocks, using their single foot like a suction cup. Barnacles also avoid being swept out to sea by cementing themselves to rocks. Then, when the tide retreats, these barnacles close their shells tight to keep their wet world safely inside. Clams dig into the sand and wait for the water's return.

—from *Ultimate Field Trip 3: Wading into Marine Biology*
by Susan E. Goodman

B. Identify the compare-and-contrast text structure in the passage.

1. Look for a word that signals a likeness between snails and barnacles. Underline it.

2. Draw boxes around the sentences that tell how snails, barnacles, and clams avoid being drawn out to sea with the tides.

C. Write one sentence that compares snails and barnacles.

_____

_____

_____

_____

© Harcourt

Name _____

Explore: Making Clear Comparisons and Contrasts

You can use compare-and-contrast writing to describe how things are alike and different. To make clear comparisons and contrasts, you should use examples and exact details.

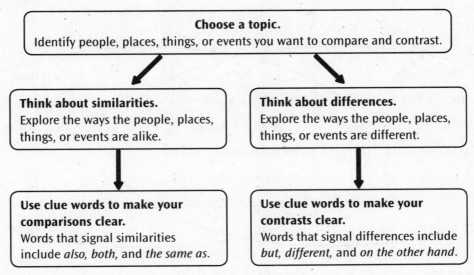

Choose a topic.
Identify people, places, things, or events you want to compare and contrast.

Think about similarities.
Explore the ways the people, places, things, or events are alike.

Think about differences.
Explore the ways the people, places, things, or events are different.

Use clue words to make your comparisons clear.
Words that signal similarities include *also, both,* and *the same as*.

Use clue words to make your contrasts clear.
Words that signal differences include *but, different,* and *on the other hand*.

A. Read each sentence and underline the people, places, things, or events being compared or contrasted. Write whether the sentence compares or contrasts and draw a box around clue words.

> **Example** In autumn leaves change color, but in springtime flowers bloom. contrast

1. Coniferous forests and deciduous forests are both home to a variety of animals. _____

2. A ballet recital is similar to a piano recital in that students perform what they have learned for an audience. _____

3. Unlike insects, spiders have eight legs. _____

B. Read this paragraph from *Ultimate Field Trip 3: Wading into Marine Biology*. On the lines below, write what is being compared and contrasted.

> Winter can turn the small tide pool icy cold. The summer sun makes it too hot for comfort. And, as the temperature rises, oxygen bubbles out of the water, leaving less for animals to breathe. A tide pool's water can evaporate, too, making the water that remains much too salty. Rain can make the water not salty enough.

_____

_____

Name _____

Use: Clear Comparisons and Contrasts

A good **compare-and-contrast composition** states how things are similar and different. Before you write a composition that compares and contrasts, you should organize your thoughts and information. Here is how one student started to think about two story characters.

Example

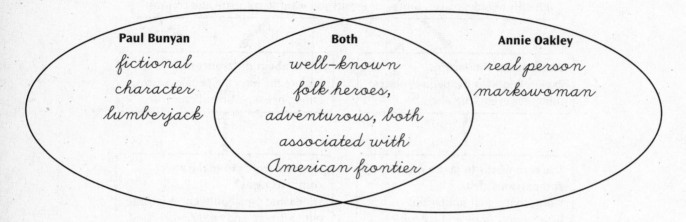

Paul Bunyan
fictional
character
lumberjack

Both
well-known
folk heroes,
adventurous, both
associated with
American frontier

Annie Oakley
real person
markswoman

A. Think about two characters from stories you have read. What qualities do the characters have in common? What qualities are unique to each? Complete the graphic organizer to compare and contrast the characters.

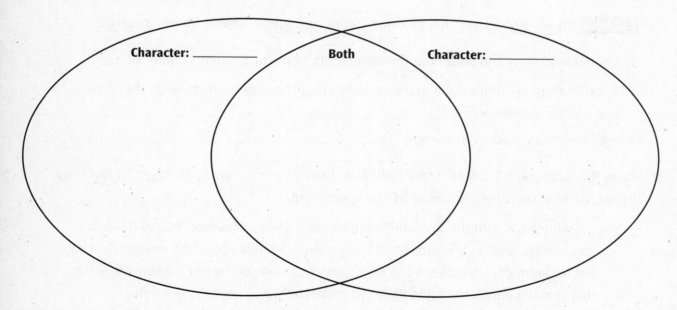

Character: _____   Both   Character: _____

B. Use your completed graphic organizer to write a draft of a short compare-and-contrast composition. Write it on another sheet of paper.

Name _____

The Parts of a Compare-and-Contrast Composition

In a **compare-and-contrast composition**, effective writers do not just say that two things are alike or different—they use details to support their statements. Below is a compare-and-contrast composition written by a fifth grader. As you read it, think about how the student organized it. Then answer the questions.

Student Model

DRAFT

Paul Bunyan and Annie Oakley
by Tyler

Paul Bunyan and Annie Oakley are two well-known characters in American folklore. Initially, there does not seem to be much more similarity between them. A lumberjack of enormous size and great strength, Paul Bunyan is a fictional character. In contrast, Annie Oakley was a small markswoman of amazing skill. She was also a real person.

However, these characters are alike in several ways. Both Paul Bunyan and Annie Oakley are described as adventurous and free-spirited. They are also subjects of famous tall tales. The tales told about each character are funny, entertaining, and teach people things. In addition, Paul Bunyan and Annie Oakley both symbolize the American frontier and American values.

> **Introduce** your topic.

> **Make** your comparisons and contrasts clear. Organize your composition by grouping similarities together and differences together.

> **Develop** your ideas by adding details that support your points.

> **Include** words that signal a comparison or a contrast.

> **Write** a concluding sentence about both.

1. Which sentence introduces the topic? Underline it.
2. Which paragraph compares? Place a * at its beginning.
3. Which paragraph contrasts? Place an X at its beginning.
4. What is the writer's purpose for this composition?

_____

_____

_____

Name _____

Evaluate a Compare-and-Contrast Composition

When you evaluate a compare-and-contrast composition, ask yourself how clear
the comparisons and contrasts were. You should also consider whether the
writer gave details to support the comparisons or contrasts.

Now use the checklist to evaluate the Student Model. Put a check in the box
next to each thing the writer did well. If you do not think the writer did a good
job, do not check the box.

☐ The writer introduced the topic.
☐ The writer made clear comparisons and contrasts.
☐ The similarities and differences were well organized.
☐ The writer used details to support the main idea.
☐ The writer included words that signal comparisons and words that signal contrasts.

Writer's Grammar
Singular and Plural Nouns

A *singular noun* refers to one person, place, thing, or idea. Plural nouns refer to more than one
noun. Following are the rules for how to change singular nouns into plural nouns.

Rules for Forming Plural Nouns	Examples	
1. The plural of a noun is usually formed by adding –s to a singular noun.	cat cats	field fields
2. Nouns ending in s, x, z, ch, sh, and most nouns ending in o form the plural by adding –es.	dress dresses	hero heroes
3. Some nouns ending in f or fe form the plural by changing –f or –fe to –ves.	knife knives	calf calves
4. Nouns ending in y preceded by a vowel form the plural by adding –s; nouns ending in a consonant + y form the plural by changing y to –ies.	day days	lady ladies
5. Some nouns are irregular.	person people	foot feet
6. Some nouns have no singular form. Others are always singular.	pants pants	sugar sugar

Underline the nouns in each sentence. If the noun is singular, write its plural form.
If the noun is plural, write its singular form.

1. The child said she saw a deer run into the field. _____

2. The woman put the corn on a shelf. _____

3. My puppy lost its first tooth last week. _____

© Harcourt

Name _____

Revise: Creating Parallel Phrasing

One thing the writer might have done better is to use parallel phrasing in his sentences. This means using the same kind of phrasing to express equal ideas. Here is an example of how the Student Model can be improved.

Example **Not Parallel:**

The tales told about each character are funny, entertaining, and teach people things.

Parallel:

The tales told about each character are funny, entertaining, and educational.

A. **Revise these sentences by creating parallel phrasing.**

1. I like writing poetry, drawing pictures, and to play music.

_____

_____

2. I knew that Paul Bunyan had enormous feet but not about his footsteps creating the 10,000 lakes of Minnesota.

_____

_____

3. Annie Oakley was a skilled hunter, sharpshooter, and she liked performing.

_____

_____

B. **Revise the draft you wrote on page 76. Use parallel phrasing to make your comparisons and contrasts clear. Use another sheet of paper to revise your draft.**

© Harcourt

Name _____

Identify: Using Precise Nouns and Verbs

In order to communicate successfully to their readers, writers use **precise nouns**
and **verbs.** Precise nouns and verbs are chosen carefully. They are the exact
nouns and verbs that will help readers better understand the people, places,
events, or ideas the writers describe.

A. Read this passage from *Stormalong*. Notice how the writer uses precise words to help readers
picture the boat's enormous size.

Literature Model

Soon Stormy and *The Courser* were taking cargoes all over the world—to India,
China, and Europe. It took four weeks to get all hands on deck. Teams of white horses
carried sailors from stem to stern. The ship's towering masts had to be hinged to let the
sun and moon go by. The tips of the masts were padded so they wouldn't punch holes
in the sky. The trip to the crow's nest took so long, the sailors who climbed to the top
returned with gray beards. The vessel was so big that once, when she hit an island in the
Caribbean Sea, she knocked it clear into the Gulf of Mexico!

—from *Stormalong*
by Mary Pope Osborne

B. Identify the precise nouns and verbs used in the passage.
1. Underline the nouns and verbs that tell exactly how the boat was protected so it would not
   damage the sky.
2. Draw a box around the words that describe how sailors looked when they returned from a
   trip to the crow's nest.
3. Circle the nouns and verbs that describe precisely what happened when the ship sailed in
   the Caribbean Sea.

C. What do the precise nouns and verbs in the third sentence tell you about the ship?
Write a sentence that explains.

_____

_____

_____

Name _____

A Closer Look at Writer's Craft

Explore: Using Precise Nouns and Verbs

Precise nouns and verbs help writers entertain and inform. You can use precise nouns and verbs to help readers picture an exact place or to understand a character's feelings.

> **Precise Words**
> The word *precise* means exact. Precise words give readers a much better understanding of a writer's ideas than general words do.

Nouns	
General	**Precise**
container	jug
bird	falcon
chair	throne

Verbs	
General	**Precise**
moved	trembled
look	glare
speaking	whispering

A. **Read each sentence. Then rewrite it using precise nouns and verbs to change the general description into a specific one.**

Example An insect moved across the ground. → *A spider crept across the pile of leaves.*

1. The child gave the ball to another player.

   _____

2. The animals made noises before running away.

   _____

   _____

3. They found a lot of stuff in the trash.

   _____

   _____

   _____

B. **Read this paragraph from *Stormalong*. Fill in the blanks with precise nouns and verbs.**

Stormy _____ through the _____ of _____ and _____.
He _____ through the _____ of _____ and the _____ of
_____. He _____ the _____ Mountains and _____ on
_____ down the _____ River.

81

Name _____

Use: Using Precise Nouns and Verbs

When you write a **descriptive paragraph** about a character, you focus on that person's individual traits. One way to do this is to tell an anecdote, or short story, about the person that illustrates the characteristics you want to describe. Before you write, you should choose some precise nouns and verbs that will help you tell the anecdote and describe the character accurately. Here is how one student started to think about planning a character sketch.

Example Person: _Uncle Max_   Anecdote: _my visit to workshop_

Trait 1: *messy*	Trait 2: *energetic*	Trait 3: *supportive*
Examples: *trash in workshop*	**Examples:** *quick movements*	**Examples:** *helps me practice for play*
Specific Nouns and Verbs: *piles of paper, lumber, and recycling*	**Specific Nouns and Verbs:** *flings arms, knocks over bucket*	**Specific Nouns and Verbs:** *encourages, cheers*

A. Think of someone you know well. What characteristics or personality traits would you list to describe this person? Complete the graphic organizer.

Person: _____   Anecdote: _____

Trait 1:	Trait 2:	Trait 3:
Examples:	Examples:	Examples:
Specific Nouns and Verbs:	Specific Nouns and Verbs:	Specific Nouns and Verbs:

B. Use your completed graphic organizer to write a paragraph describing someone you know very well. Write your paragraph on another sheet of paper.

Name _____

The Parts of a Descriptive Paragraph

A good **descriptive paragraph** about a person is like a good snap shot—it shows a clear and detailed image of that individual. Below is a descriptive paragraph written by a fifth-grade student. As you read it, think of how the student organized it. Then answer the questions.

Student Model

DRAFT

Uncle Max
by Ana

 The litter in the doorway is the first thing I see when I open the door to Uncle Max's workshop. I am kicking aside old junk as Uncle Max walks over to greet me. He flings his strong arms around me with such enthusiasm that he knocks over a container sitting on a nearby shelf. His brown eyes crinkling with laughter, Uncle Max shrugs his shoulders at the mess and takes my hand. Uncle Max leads me around the workshop, excitedly talking about his recent woodworking projects. When I mention that I have a part in the school play, Uncle Max encourages me to say my monologue for him. He cheers loudly when I finish. All too soon, it's time to go. Stepping over piles of paper, lumber, and recycling, I walk to the door and wave goodbye.

> **Provide** a setting for your character.

> **Show**, do not tell. Rather than name the character's traits, illustrate them by describing his or her words, actions, feelings, or physical characteristics.

> **Organize** events and details in a clear and proper sequence.

> **Choose** your words carefully. Include precise nouns and verbs.

1. Which sentence introduces the setting? Underline it.
2. What precise nouns and verbs does the writer use? Write an example of each.

 nouns: _____   verbs: _____

3. What details does the writer use to describe her uncle? Write three details on the lines below.

_____

_____

4. What does the paragraph reveal about Uncle Max?

_____

_____

© Harcourt

Evaluate a Descriptive Paragraph

When you evaluate a descriptive paragraph of a character, ask yourself how well the writer established the person's traits and characteristics.

Now use the checklist to evaluate the Student Model. Put a check in the box next to each thing the writer did well. If you do not think the writer did a good job, do not check the box.

☐ The writer described the character within an appropriate setting.
☐ The writer illustrated, rather than told, the character's traits.
☐ The events and details flowed in an order that made sense.
☐ The writer used precise nouns and verbs.

Writer's Grammar
Possessive Nouns

A possessive noun shows ownership.
The possessive form of singular nouns is formed by adding an *apostrophe* and an *s*.

Example   the food of the dog   the dog's food

The possessive form of plural nouns is formed by adding an *apostrophe*. If the plural noun does not end in *s*, then an *apostrophe* and an *s* are added.

Example   the food of the dogs   the dogs' food
              the books of the women   the women's books

Read each sentence. Rewrite the underlined word group as a possessive noun.

1. The Environmental Protection Agency is checking the water of the city.

_____

2. When they went outside, they saw that the wheels of the trucks were flat.

_____

3. The howling of the wolf woke up the entire camp last night.

_____

4. The children of the Smiths know all of the lyrics to the song.

_____

© Harcourt

Name _____

Revise: Adding Precise Nouns and Verbs

One thing the writer might have done better is to use more precise nouns and verbs. Here is an example of how the Student Model can be improved.

Example I am kicking aside old junk as Uncle Max walks over to greet me.

> *I am kicking aside a week-old pizza box as Uncle Max strides over to greet me.*

A. Revise these sentences by adding precise nouns and verbs. Use the Word Bank to help you.

1. Daryl put his stuff in his bag.

_____

_____

2. The children ate their dinner.

_____

_____

3. Looking over her shoulder, Gertrude saw something.

_____

_____

Word Bank

cram
gulp
garden
souvenir
suitcase

B. Revise the draft you wrote on page 82. Add precise nouns and verbs to make a clear mental picture for readers. Use another sheet of paper if you need more space.

_____

_____

_____

_____

_____

© Harcourt

Writer's Companion • UNIT 3
Lesson 13 *Using Precise Nouns and Verbs*

Name _____

Review Writer's Craft

Skilled writers focus on sentence fluency by beginning sentences with different structures and by choosing interesting words. When comparing or contrasting, good writers make sure all details are clear. They can do this by choosing precise nouns and verbs.

A. Read the passage below. Notice how the writer uses a variety of sentence beginnings and precise nouns and verbs to make his writing clear and appealing.

Literature Model

When water cools, it loses energy. The molecules slow down and eventually stop swirling and pushing each other. When water freezes, the molecules lock together, forming a rigid structure. A drop of blue water no longer moves. The water has changed from a liquid to a solid—ice.

Ice is a solid, like metal or rock. But, unlike metal or rock, ice is solid only at temperatures of 32 degrees Fahrenheit (0 degrees Celsius) or colder. At room temperature, ice melts, changing back to a liquid.

—from *A Drop of Water*
by Walter Wick

B. Review how the writer expresses ideas.

1. Look for different sentence beginnings. Underline a sentence that begins with a prepositional phrase.

2. Look for precise nouns and verbs. Circle two specific nouns and two specific verbs.

3. Draw a box around a sentence that compares. Which word signals the comparison? _____

C. What is the main idea of the passage?

_____

_____

_____

_____

© Harcourt

Name _____

Review Writer's Craft

Sentence fluency and **word choice** make a writer's ideas easier to recognize and understand. They also make the writing more enjoyable to read.

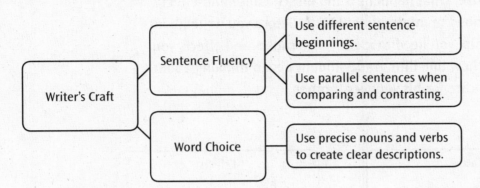

A. Read this passage from *A Drop of Water*. Notice how the writer develops sentence fluency and uses good word choice.

> All of the snowflakes on this page were photographed on the same day. All share the same angles, but vary in design. One has six branches of unequal length, giving the appearance of a three-sided snowflake. Another snowflake has only four branches. Apparently, two of its branches didn't grow. Odd variations like these are typical. Because different conditions of humidity, wind, and temperature affected the growth of each snowflake as it fell, each design holds the secrets of it unique journey to earth.
>
> When a snowflake melts, its intricate design is lost forever in a drop of water. But a snowflake can vanish in another way. It can change directly from ice to vapor.

B. For each sentence, tell how the writer begins the sentence. Then write one precise noun and one precise verb from each sentence.

Example Apparently, two of its branches didn't grow.

begins with a single word; branches, grow

1. All of the photographs on this page were photographed on the same day.

_____

2. When a snowflake melts, its intricate design is lost forever in a drop of water.

_____

Name _____

Review Writer's Craft

When you write a **cause-and-effect paragraph**, you tell about the relationship between events, actions, or behavior. The event, action, or behavior that makes something happen is the **cause**. What happens is the **effect**. Cause-and-effect relationships are often described in informational texts. Before you write about a cause-and-effect relationship, you need to identify the causes and effects you want to write about. Here is how one fifth-grade student began thinking about explaining the effects of day care for his younger brother.

Example

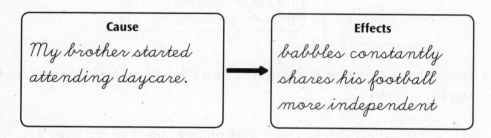

Cause		Effects
My brother started attending daycare.	→	babbles constantly shares his football more independent

A. Use the graphic organizer above to answer the following questions.

1. What topic has the writer chosen for his cause-and-effect paragraph?

_____

2. What precise nouns and verbs does the student use?

_____

_____

3. What other effects might daycare have had on the student's brother?

_____

4. Use the information listed in the graphic organizer. Write a good beginning sentence for the paragraph.

_____

_____

© Harcourt

Name _____

The Parts of a Cause-and-Effect Paragraph

A **cause-and-effect paragraph** describes the reasons for or the results of a situation or event. In text, a cause-and-effect relationship is often signaled by words such as *because, so, since,* and *as a result*. Below is an example of a cause-and-effect paragraph written by a fifth-grade student. As you read it, think about how the student organized it. Then answer the questions.

Student Model

DRAFT

Daycare for Donald
by Eddie

Since he started daycare, my brother Donald has changed in many ways. For one thing, he has learned many new words. Before he started daycare, Donald knew a few simple words, and he didn't talk very much. Now his vocabulary is much larger, and he babbles constantly! Another result of Donald being in daycare is that he has become more independent. Donald used to cry whenever my parents left us with a sitter. In contrast, these days he hugs them goodbye without a single tear and goes on playing. Daycare has also taught Donald how to get along with other children. In the past, he clung to his football around them. But his teachers at the daycare center stressed the importance of sharing. As a result, Donald has learned to play well in a group and share his football easily.

Introduce the topic of the paragraph by stating the cause (or the effect) you are writing about.

Describe the cause-and-effect relationship using details and examples. Include words that signal causes and effects.

Use different sentence beginnings and precise nouns and verbs to make your writing interesting and clear.

1. Which sentence introduces the topic of the paragraph? Circle it.
2. Which words does the writer use to signal cause-and-effect relationships? Underline two of them.
3. What is the stated cause in this paragraph?

_____

4. What are three effects or results of the cause?

_____

_____

_____

Name _____

Evaluate a Cause-and-Effect Paragraph

A. Two students were asked to write a cause-and-effect paragraph about a landform. The paragraph below got a score of 4. When using a 4-point rubric, a score of 4 means "excellent." Read the paragraph and teacher comments. Find out why this cause-and-effect paragraph is a success.

Student Model

Three Ways to Make an Island
by Pete

Have you ever thought about how islands form? There are three main types of islands, and they are formed in three different ways. Continental islands are portions of land that were once connected to a continent. When melting ice caps raise the level of the seas, land connected to a continent is cut off and becomes an island. Volcanic islands form when a mountain rises from the sea. Like volcanoes on land, underwater volcanoes release lava when they erupt. With each eruption, lava builds up and the mountain gets taller. Over time, the volcano grows above the surface of the water, forming a volcanic island. Coral islands begin with colonies of ocean animals called polyps. Polyps build limestone walls around their bodies for protection. As the colony grows, so do the limestone walls. As a result, reefs that cover hundreds of square miles develop. When the sea drops or land below the reef rises, the reef emerges from the water. Sand and dust gather on the reef, and an island forms.

> Great! You introduced your topic with an interesting sentence to draw in your readers.

> You did an excellent job varying your sentence beginnings and using precise vocabulary.

> You did a good job using words to signal cause-and-effect relationships for the reader.

> Your cause-and-effect paragraph is well thought out and very clear. You introduced an effect (formation of islands) and discussed several different causes. Good work!

B. This summary got a score of 2. Why did it get a low score?

Student Model

How Rivers Form
by Ellie

Rivers form over a long period of time. Water flows from higher places to lower places. Here is the series of actions that make them. Rain falls on mountains, and sometimes it collects in depressions in the rocks. When it gets cold, the water freezes, and erosion occurs. Water continues to wear away rock over time. Wind and weather does, too. After some time, small streams form. The streams cause further erosion. The stream grows larger and becomes a river.

> Focus your introductory sentence. A cause-and-effect relationship is not set up here.

> Are the causes and effects clear? You could use signal words and vary your sentence beginnings more to help readers follow the flow of ideas.

> Good work including the term *depressions*. But what kind of weather erodes rock? You could use more precise vocabulary to help readers understand these processes better.

C. What score would you give the student's paragraph? Put a number on each line.

	4	3	2	1
Sentence Fluency _____	☐ There is a lot of variety in sentence beginnings, and the writer uses many precise nouns and verbs.	☐ There is some variety in sentence beginnings, and the writer uses some precise nouns and verbs.	☐ There is almost no variety in sentence beginnings, but the writer uses some precise nouns and verbs.	☐ There is little or no variety in sentence beginnings, and the vocabulary is lacking in precision.
Conventions _____	☐ The writer uses a clear, correct cause-and-effect paragraph structure with strong reasons and results.	☐ The writer uses a clear, correct cause-and-effect paragraph structure with some reasons and results.	☐ The cause-and-effect structure is clear but there are not enough reasons and results.	☐ The cause-and-effect structure is unclear and there are little or no reasons and results.
Word Choice _____	☐ The writer always uses precise nouns and verbs.	☐ The writer usually uses precise nouns and verbs.	☐ The writer uses some precise nouns and verbs.	☐ The writer does not use precise nouns and verbs.

© Harcourt

Name _____

Extended Writing/Test Prep

On the first two pages of this lesson, you will use what you have learned about different kinds of paragraphs to write a longer written work.

A. **Read the three choices below. Put a star by the writing activity you would like to do.**

1. Respond to a Writing Prompt.

Writing Situation: A friend tells you that she doesn't think her poor eating habits and lack of exercise affect her overall health that much.

Directions for Writing: Think about what you know about being healthy. Now, write a cause-and-effect essay that shows how healthy eating and exercise affect people. Remember to use different sentence beginnings and precise nouns and verbs in your essay.

2. Choose one of the pieces of writing you started in this unit:

- a descriptive paragraph, setting (page 70)
- a compare-and-contrast composition (page 76)
- a descriptive paragraph, character (page 82)

Revise and expand your work into a complete piece of writing. Use what you have learned about sentence fluency and word choice to help readers understand the people, places, events, or ideas you write about.

3. Choose a topic you would like to write about. Write a cause-and-effect essay to describe a cause-and-effect relationship with which you are familiar.

B. **Use the space below and on the next page to plan your writing.**

TOPIC: _____

WRITING FORM: _____

HOW I WILL ORGANIZE MY WRITING: _____

_____

_____

_____

_____

© Harcourt

Name _____

C. In the space below, draw a graphic organizer that will help you plan your writing. Fill in the graphic organizer. Write additional notes on the lines below.

Notes

_____

_____

_____

_____

_____

_____

_____

D. Do your writing on another sheet of paper.

Name _____

Answering Multiple-Choice Questions

For questions on pages 94–97, fill in the bubble next to the correct answer.

A. Daisy made the Venn Diagram below to organize ideas for a paper. Use her diagram to answer questions 1–3.

Daisy's Venn Diagram

Venus　　　　**Both**　　　　**Earth**

no water, carbon dioxide, no life, highest temperature is 864 degrees Fahrenheit

similar in size, mass, and gravity, nitrogen in atmosphere, about the same distance from the sun

water, oxygen, life, highest temperature is 136 degrees Fahrenheit

1. Based on the information in Daisy's Venn Diagram, what kind of paper is Daisy planning to write?

   (A)　a paper that tells a story about Earth and Venus

   (B)　a paper that describes the solar system

   (C)　a paper that explains how Earth and Venus were formed

   (D)　a paper that compares and contrasts Earth and Venus

Test Tip:
The center of a Venn Diagram lists features that are shared by the subjects listed in the outer sections.

2. According to the diagram, which characteristic do the planets share?

   (A)　They both have nitrogen in their atmospheres.

   (B)　They both have oxygen in their atmospheres.

   (C)　They both have carbon dioxide in their atmospheres.

   (D)　They both have helium in their atmospheres.

3. Based on the information in Daisy's diagram, which of the following details should NOT be added to the center section of the diagram?

   (A)　The density of Venus is about the same as Earth's.

   (B)　Earth has one moon, but Venus has no moons.

   (C)　Like Earth, Venus has volcanoes.

   (D)　Both planets have few craters.

Name _____

B. The descriptive paragraph below is a first draft that Bernie wrote. The paragraph needs some changes. Read the paragraph to answer questions 1–3.

The Parade

(1) Sequins sparkle in the sunlight as the dancers leap and twirl. (2) The wind blows the smell of crisp fall leaves down the street. (3) The members of the marching band raise their instruments and smile at the crowd. (4) A whistle sounds. (5) The bass drum slowly pounds out a beat. (6) Everyone cheers loudly as the shiny brass trumpets join in the tune. (7) Brass is a metal made from zinc and copper. (8) The flashing blue and gold flags catch my eye as the band moves proudly down the street. (9) Before it is out of sight, the next band comes into view.

1. Which sentence is off topic and should be taken out of the paragraph?
   - (A) sentence (2)
   - (B) sentence (4)
   - (C) sentence (7)
   - (D) sentence (8)

> **Test Tip:**
> Different sentence beginnings makes writing interesting. One way to change sentence beginnings is to change the order of the words from the original sentence.

2. The writer wants to add the following sentence to the paragraph:

   > **When the yelling stops, I hear the cheerful music play on.**

   Where should this sentence be added to keep the events in order?
   - (A) after sentence (3)
   - (B) after sentence (5)
   - (C) after sentence (6)
   - (D) after sentence (9)

3. Which shows the best way to revise sentence (5) to make the beginning different?
   - (A) The drum, which was bass, slowly pounds out a beat.
   - (B) Pounding, the bass drum beats slow.
   - (C) The slow beat of the bass drum pounds.
   - (D) Slowly, the brass drum pounds out a beat.

C. Read the paragraph. Choose the word or words that correctly complete questions 1–4.

What's that Noise?

Loud creaking in my ___(1)___ house always frightened me, until I found out there was a harmless explanation. My mother told me that the strange noises were just the sounds of the house settling down for the night. She explained that during the day, the ___(2)___ warms up. Materials in the house, such as wooden floorboards, expanded when they were heated. Then, as it got darker, the temperature dropped. The house cooled off, and the materials in the house shrank. The results of the expanding and shrinking were the noises I heard—creaks, pops, and squeaks. The reason I heard the noises at night was that the sounds of everyday ___(3)___ had quieted down. My mother's explanation made me feel better, but I still think there are ___(4)___ in the attic!

1. Which answer should go in blank (1)?
   Ⓐ families
   Ⓑ family's
   Ⓒ familie

2. Which answer should go in blank (2)?
   Ⓐ house
   Ⓑ houses
   Ⓒ house's

3. Which answer should go in blank (3)?
   Ⓐ activitys
   Ⓑ activity's
   Ⓒ activities

4. Which answer should go in blank (4)?
   Ⓐ mice
   Ⓑ mouses
   Ⓒ mice's

> **Test Tip:**
> Plural nouns name more than one person, place or thing.
> Possessive nouns show ownership.

© Harcourt

Name _____

D. Read and answer questions 1–4.

1. In which sentence below is all **capitalization** correct?
   - (A) Esther went to the grand canyon last summer.
   - (B) Esther went to the Grand canyon last summer.
   - (C) Esther went to the Grand Canyon last summer.

2. In which sentence below is all **capitalization** correct?
   - (A) Aunt Judy is taking me to see the American Ballet Theater.
   - (B) Aunt Judy is taking me to see the American Ballet theater.
   - (C) Aunt judy taking me to see the american ballet theater.

3. In which sentence below is all **capitalization** correct?
   - (A) Is your birthday on Monday or Tuesday this Year?
   - (B) Is your birthday on Monday or Tuesday this year?
   - (C) Is your birthday on monday or tuesday this year?

> **Test Tip:**
> Common nouns are not capitalized unless they begin a sentence, are part of a title, or begin a direct quotation.
>
> Proper nouns name particular places, people, or things, and are always capitalized.

4. In which sentence below is all **capitalization** correct?
   - (A) The representative from New jersey is a member of congress.
   - (B) The Representative from New jersey is a member of congress.
   - (C) The representative from New Jersey is a member of Congress.

5. In which sentence below is all **capitalization** correct?
   - (A) I have Professor Yamamoto for my course in japanese.
   - (B) I have Professor Yamamoto for my course in Japanese.
   - (C) I have professor Yamamoto for my course in Japanese.

© Harcourt

Name _____

Identify: Sensory Details

Sensory details are words that appeal to the senses of sight, sound, taste, smell, and touch. Writers use sensory details to help readers share thoughts, feelings, and experiences.

A. Read the following passage. Notice how the writer uses sensory details to describe the different animals.

Literature Model

"What would you like in exchange for the stories?" Anansi asked the Ruler.

The Ruler contemplated Anansi's request. Then the skies lightened at his smile, for he knew the payment he wanted was difficult to acquire. "Bring me Onini, the python with the devastating squeeze; Osebo, the panther with the spearlike teeth; and the Mmoboro, the hornets whose stings ache like fire."

Anansi bowed and journeyed home to gather the payment.

Anansi collected a long branch and a coil of vines and went to the stream where Onini rested. Back and forth Anansi strolled in front of the python, all the time chuckling with satisfaction.

—from *How Anansi Gave the World Stories*
Folktale

B. Identify sensory details in the passage.

1. Underline at least two words or phrases that appeal to the sense of sight.
2. Circle at least one word or phrase that appeals to the sense of touch.
3. Draw a box around the word or phrase that appeals to the sense of sound.

C. What sensory details does the writer use to describe Onini, Osebo, and Mmoboro? Why do you think the writer uses these details?

_____

_____

_____

_____

Name _____

Explore: Sensory Details

Sensory details can paint vivid pictures in readers' minds. This helps make writing more lively and entertaining for the readers.

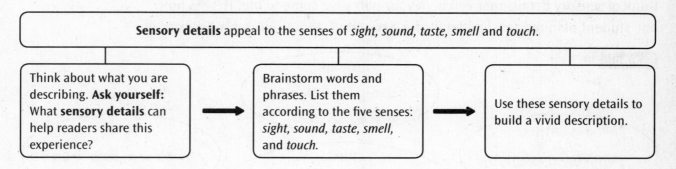

Sensory details appeal to the senses of *sight, sound, taste, smell* and *touch*.

Think about what you are describing. **Ask yourself:** What **sensory details** can help readers share this experience?

→

Brainstorm words and phrases. List them according to the five senses: *sight, sound, taste, smell, and touch.*

→

Use these sensory details to build a vivid description.

A. Read each sentence below. Circle the word or words that appeal to the sense in parentheses.

Example The crows on the telephone line (loudly squawked) at the cat on the sidewalk. (sound)

1. The bright pink band of sunburn on my shoulder burned and itched all morning. (touch)

2. The cats meowed at the trashcan because of its fishy odor. (smell)

3. I ran so hard that salty sweat dripped down my face and into my mouth. (taste)

4. My dog Felix whimpered when he heard the thundering booms of the fireworks. (sound)

5. The moth fluttered in arcs and circles around the light. (sight)

B. Read this passage from *How Anansi Gave the World Stories.* Underline the sensory details.

> The hornets thought themselves clever creatures indeed. They did not want Anansi to be dry while they were soaking wet, so they swarmed into the gourd. They buzzed. "You were mistaken to think we weren't clever. Now we shall stay dry."

C. Suppose it is summer and you are walking in your neighborhood. Write a sentence that describes the scene. Use sensory details that appeal to at least three of the five senses.

_____

_____

_____

© Harcourt

Name _____

Use: Sensory Details

A **narrative** tells a story using characters, setting, and a plot. Some narratives
are based on real events, and others are made up. Before you write a narrative,
think of sensory details that will help your narrative come to life. Here is how
one student planned sensory details for a narrative about riding a roller coaster.

Example

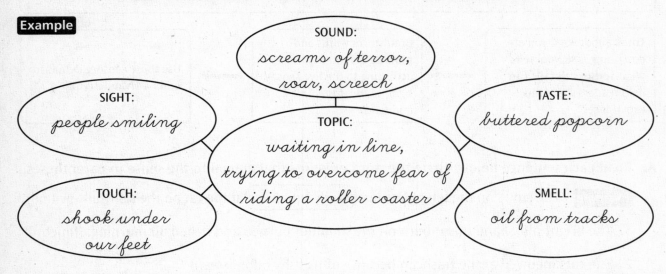

SOUND: screams of terror, roar, screech

SIGHT: people smiling

TOPIC: waiting in line, trying to overcome fear of riding a roller coaster

TASTE: buttered popcorn

TOUCH: shook under our feet

SMELL: oil from tracks

A. Think of a time that you or someone you know did something that was a challenge. Identify
the challenge in the topic bubble. Then use the web to brainstorm sensory details that will
make the experience come alive for your readers.

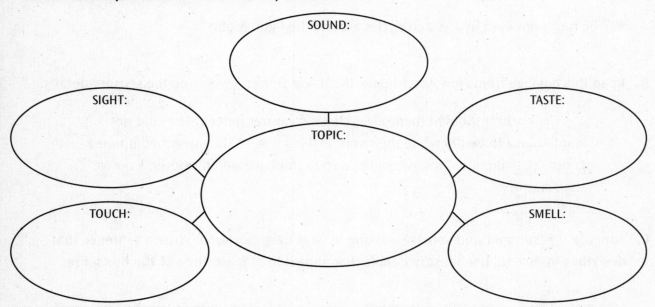

SOUND:

SIGHT:

TOPIC:

TASTE:

TOUCH:

SMELL:

B. Use the sensory details in your web to write a narrative about meeting a challenge. Use
dialogue and sensory details to make your narrative more true to life. Write your draft on
another sheet of paper.

Name _____

The Parts of a Narrative Paragraph

Here is an example of a **narrative paragraph** written by a fifth grader. As you read, think about how the student organized it. Then answer the questions.

Student Model

DRAFT

Ms. Jitters
by María

I ducked at the screams of terror and the roar of the roller coaster as it barreled above our heads. The platform shook under our feet. "A little nervous, Ms. Jitters?" Francine joked, pointing to my hand. I was biting my nails. I could taste buttered popcorn on my fingertips. But even that sweet, salty taste could not make me forget how nervous roller coasters made me feel. A man was selling balloons. Francine and I were the first in line, waiting for the next car to screech onto the platform and carry us off into the sky. Francine asked, "What is there to be afraid of?" It was a simple question, but I could not think of a good answer before our car arrived. The people who were stepping out of the car were smiling. "Maybe nothing," I sighed, as I found my seat in the car. "I'm sure everything will be just fine."

Introduce the topic with a dramatic event that catches readers' interest.

Organize ideas in time order.

Focus by telling only the events that related to your narrative.

Develop your narrative. Use *dialogue* to make it lively. Use *sensory details* that will let readers share the experience.

Conclude with an interesting event or comment.

1. Which sentence introduces the topic? Underline it.
2. Which sentence does not relate to the point of the narrative? Draw a line through it.
3. Which sentence concludes the narrative? Draw a box around it.
4. What does the dialogue tell you about Francine?

_____

_____

5. Find the sensory details. Write an example of each type of detail below.

Sight: _____

Sound: _____

Touch: _____

Taste: _____

Evaluate a Narrative Paragraph

When you evaluate a narrative paragraph, ask yourself how well the writer communicated the experience. Also ask yourself how well the writer used sensory details to help you picture the scene.

Now evaluate the Student Model. Put a check beside each thing the writer has done well. If you do not think the writer did a good job, do not check the box.

☐ The writer captured readers' interest by introducing the topic with a dramatic event.

☐ The writer organized the narrative in time order.

☐ The writer focused the narrative by telling only events that related to the topic.

☐ The writer developed the narrative with dialogue and sensory details.

☐ The writer concluded with an interesting event or comment.

Writer's Grammar
Subject and Object Pronouns

A **subject pronoun** takes the place of a noun, or nouns, in the subject of a sentence.

> *Singular Subject Pronouns:* I, you, he, she, it
> *Plural Subject Pronouns:* we, you, they

Example **I** ate the last piece of pizza. **They** gave Tim some pizza.

An **object pronoun** takes the place of a noun that comes after an action verb or preposition.

> *Singular Object Pronouns:* me, you, him, her, it
> *Plural Object Pronouns:* us, you, them

Example Tim gave **me** the last piece of pizza. Mark and Emily share the pizza with **us**.

Circle the pronoun that correctly completes each sentence.

1. (We, Us) decorated the wall with a mural of a rain forest.
2. He and (I, me) watched the movie from beginning to end.
3. I loaned (he, him) my bicycle for the afternoon.
4. After the heavy rains, (she, her) warned us not to go near the creek.
5. My mother offered to tell (we, us) a story if we would sit down.

© Harcourt

Name _____

Revise: Adding Sensory Details

One thing the writer could have done better is to add more sensory details. Those details would have helped her do a better job of describing the characters and narrative. Here is an example of how a sentence from the Student Model could be improved.

Example   The platform shook under our feet.

The smell of oil came from the track as the platform shook and shuddered under our feet.

A. Revise these sentences. Add sensory details that will help readers share the experience. Use the Word Bank to help you.

1. The dog walked across the floor.

   _____

2. I tried to keep myself from smelling the odor.

   _____

   _____

3. My brother bit into a slice of lemon.

   _____

   _____

4. The house looked old.

   _____

   _____

5. Her grandmother's surfboard was decorated with many colors.

   _____

   _____

Word Bank

blue
bulldog
clicked
collapse
foul
funny
panted
purple
sour
waved
wood
worn

B. Revise the draft of the narrative you wrote on page 100. Add sensory details to make the sentences more descriptive and entertaining for readers. Also pay close attention to subject and object pronouns. Write your revision on another sheet of paper.

© Harcourt

Name _____

Identify: Creating Specific Voices

Writers make story characters seem real by giving each character his or her own voice. These voices help show readers what the characters are like. Writers build their characters' voices by using dialogue and descriptive words.

A. Read this passage. Notice how the writer creates different voices for the characters.

Literature Model

Out of the door of Eva's building came Mr. Sims, the actor, carrying his enormous cat, Oliver. Mr. Sims was "on hiatus again," which meant out of work, in between shows, and so, every day, dressed in his finest, he embarked on a daily promenade with Olivier under his arm. "Writing?" he asked.

"Trying to," Eva answered, "but nothing ever happens on 90th Street!"

"You are mistaken, my dear," Mr. Sims said. "The whole world's a stage—even 90th Street—and each of us plays a part. Watch the stage, observe the players carefully, and don't neglect the details," he said, stroking Olivier. "Follow an old actor's advice and you will find you have plenty to write about."

—from *Nothing Ever Happens on 90th Street*
by Roni Schotter

B. Identify how the writer gives each character his or her own specific voice.
1. Circle the part of the dialogue that shows what Eva is like.
2. Underline the part of the dialogue that shows what Mr. Sims is like.
3. In your own words, tell what Mr. Sims is like.

_____

_____

C. What do you think Eva might say in reply to Mr. Sims? Remember to put the words in Eva's voice.

_____

_____

© Harcourt

Name _____

Explore: Creating Specific Voices

Writers create a **specific voice** for each character in a story or play.

Specific voices bring characters to life.	**Specific voices** show how each character is unique.	**Specific voices** show how each character thinks or feels.

A. Read each sentence of dialogue below. Put a check to show which character said the words. Underline the word or words that help create a specific voice for that character.

> **Example** "I'm all <u>revved up</u> and <u>ready to roll</u>!"
>
> ✓ Mr. Henry: a bus driver who is easily excited
>
> _____ Mrs. Hernández: a lawyer who rarely smiles

1. "I'm going to hit this one out of the park."

_____ Vanessa: a student who is good at sports

_____ Theo: a student who prefers computers

2. "My thoughts branch in many directions but bloom only after I jot them down."

_____ Michelle: a doctor who likes to go rock climbing

_____ Marcus: a writer who likes plants and trees

3. "That creepy little thing put its dirty feet on my book."

_____ Jorge: an older brother who does not like mice

_____ Emma: an older sister who likes mice

B. Suppose that you are writing a story about a fifth grader who thinks her mother is going to throw a surprise picnic for her. Write at least two lines of dialogue that create a specific voice for the character.

_____

_____

_____

_____

Name _____

Use: Creating Specific Voices

A **skit** is a short play. It uses characters and dialogue to tell a story. Before you write a skit, organize your ideas so that each character has his or her own voice. Here is how one student started to plan his skit.

Example Setting: _outside_

Name of Character	*Amy*
Personality	*funny* *likes to laugh and joke with her friends*
Words that Character Might Use	*"What's up?"* *"Tell me something funny."*

A. Think about a setting and one character for a humorous skit. Then fill out the chart.

Setting: _____

Name of Character	
Personality	
Words that Character Might Use	

B. Use information from your chart to write a short, humorous skit with two or more characters. You may want to create a separate chart for each character. Then write your draft on another sheet of paper.

Name _____

The Parts of a Skit

A **skit** is a short play that can be performed for an audience. Actors read the dialogue and use movements and gestures to act out what is happening. Here is a skit written by a fifth grader. As you read it, think about how the student organized it. Then answer the questions.

Student Model

DRAFT

Looking at Something
by Dimitri

(*Ben is looking up into the sky. Amy and Kai enter.*)

Amy: Hey, Ben! What's up? (*slaps her knee and laughs*)

Ben (*still looking up*): Oh, nothing.

Kai (*to Amy*): My educated guess is that he sees something.

Tim: What are y'all looking at?

(*Amy and Kai look up also. Tim enters.*)

Amy: Ben is keeping his secret to himself.

Tim (*excited*): I think I see it!

Amy (*getting frustrated*): See what? All I see is sky!

Tim (*pointing, excited*): That hawk! Over there!

Kai (*pointing, calm*): Or maybe those cumulus clouds over there?

Ben (*smiling*): Thanks, guys! I hoped I would see something!

> Use stage directions to **introduce the *setting* and *characters*.**

> **Write the name of the character** before the words he or she speaks.

> **Develop** the skit with realistic dialogue.

> **Create a specific voice** for each character.

> Use **possessive and reflexive pronouns** correctly.

> **Conclude** with an interesting event or line of dialogue.

1. Which stage directions introduce the characters and setting? Underline them.
2. Which line of dialogue seems to be out of order? Circle it. Then draw an arrow to the place where you think the dialogue belongs.
3. What do you think Kai is like? Explain by using the descriptive words that the writer uses to create a specific voice for him.

_____

_____

Name _____

Evaluate a Skit

When you evaluate a skit, ask yourself how well the writer created specific voices for the characters.

Now evaluate the Student Model. Put a check beside each thing the writer did well. If you do not think the writer did a good job with something, do not check the box.

- ☐ The writer used stage directions to introduce the setting and characters.
- ☐ The writer wrote the name of the character before the words he or she speaks.
- ☐ The writer developed the skit with realistic dialogue.
- ☐ The writer created a specific voice for each character.
- ☐ The writer concluded with an interesting event or line of dialogue.

Writer's Grammar
Possessive and Reflexive Pronouns

A **pronoun** takes the place of one or more nouns. A **possessive pronoun** shows ownership. It takes the place of a possessive noun such as *María's* or *The boy's*. Some possessive pronouns come immediately before a noun. Others are used alone.

Possessive Pronouns Used Before a Noun	Possessive Pronouns Used Alone
Singular: my, your, his, her, its	*Singular:* mine, yours, his, hers
Plural: our, your, their	*Plural:* ours, yours, theirs

Example Tess: I thought only **my** dog was cute, but **yours** is too.

A **reflexive pronoun** refers back to a noun or pronoun in the subject.

Singular: myself, yourself, himself, herself, itself

Plural: ourselves, yourselves, themselves

Example Adam: We should give **ourselves** a big round of applause!

Complete each line of dialogue with the correct pronoun in parentheses.

1. Dina: Have you seen _____ friend Jessica? (my, mine)

2. Carl: Yes! She said she wanted to study by _____. (her, herself)

3. Dina: She's smart. We should be studying by _____, too. (ours, ourselves)

© Harcourt

Name _____

Revise: Showing Characters' Traits

One way the writer could have improved his skit is by showing the characters' traits more clearly. Writers can do this by creating a specific voice for each character. They also can include stage directions that make a characters' behavior more realistic. Here is how a line of dialogue from the Student Model could be improved.

Example Amy: Ben is keeping his secret to himself.

Amy: Super secretive Ben is keeping his super secret to himself.

(nudges Kai and laughs)

A. Revise each line of dialogue by choosing the characters' traits and then showing them more clearly. Add stage directions to show what each character does while speaking. Use the Word Bank to help you.

1. Miguel: You won't believe what I just did!

   _____

   _____

   _____

2. Zoe: I am tired.

   _____

   _____

   _____

3. Darla (*shaking her head*): No thanks. I don't like beets.

   _____

   _____

   _____

Word Bank

bushed
excitedly
exhausted
frowning
hate
running
yawning

B. Revise your skit from page 106. As you revise, make sure that you show the characters' traits clearly. Also make sure that you use possessive and reflexive pronouns correctly. Use another sheet of paper for your writing.

© Harcourt

Name _____

Identify: Vivid Words and Phrases

Writers use **vivid words and phrases** to create exact pictures of what they want to describe. Vivid words and phrases make writing lively and entertaining.

A. Read the following passage. Notice how the writer includes vivid words and phrases.

Literature Model

The caterpillar moved its head constantly. Sometimes fast, sometimes a little slower, but never stopping—it looked like really hard work. The silk came out of its mouth just as Patrick had said.

At first the silk was almost invisible. You could see the strands only if you looked really hard.

By the next morning, though, the caterpillar had already wrapped itself in a layer of silk. It looked like it was living inside a cloud. We could see its black mouth moving, moving, busy, busy, busy.

—from *Project Mulberry*
by Linda Sue Park

B. Identify vivid words and phrases in the passage.

1. Underline words and phrases in the first paragraph that describe how the caterpillar moves.

2. Circle words and phrases in the second paragraph that describe the silk.

3. Put a box around the words in the last sentence that describe the caterpillar's mouth.

C. How does the appearance of the silk change overnight? Use details from the passage to answer in your own words.

_____

_____

_____

_____

Name _____

Explore: Vivid Words and Phrases

Vivid words and phrases help readers feel as if they are actually experiencing what is being described. They make events and characters seem real.

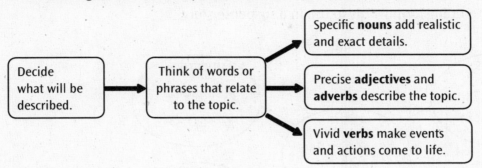

A. Read the paragraph. Then identify the vivid words and phrases.

Example Underline the vivid phrase that describes where Eduardo sees the wildflowers.

Eduardo focused his sights on the snow-capped mountain peak that towered proudly above the trees. He trudged ahead on the rocky mountain path, pausing only to inspect the timid wildflowers that were peeking <u>through the dead leaves and broken branches.</u>

1. Circle the adjective and the adverb that describe the mountain peak.
2. Put a box around at least two verbs that tell what Eduardo does.
3. What does the writer say about how the wildflowers look?

_____

_____

B. Read the passage from *Project Mulberry*. Underline the words that describe how the caterpillars move.

Some of the caterpillars sort of stood up halfway and swayed around like they were investigating their new homes. Then they coiled themselves up neatly.

C. Suppose you are observing how a particular insect moves. Write a sentence that uses vivid words and phrases to describe it.

_____

_____

Name _____

Use: Vivid Words and Phrases

A **suspense story** is a mystery in which readers are not sure what will happen.
Vivid words and phrases help make the mystery seem real for readers. Here is
how one student started to brainstorm words to use in a suspense story.

Example

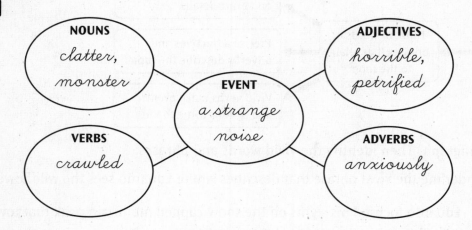

NOUNS
clatter, monster

ADJECTIVES
horrible, petrified

EVENT
a strange noise

VERBS
crawled

ADVERBS
anxiously

A. Think of a strange or mysterious event. Then use the word web to brainstorm any vivid
words and phrases that come to mind.

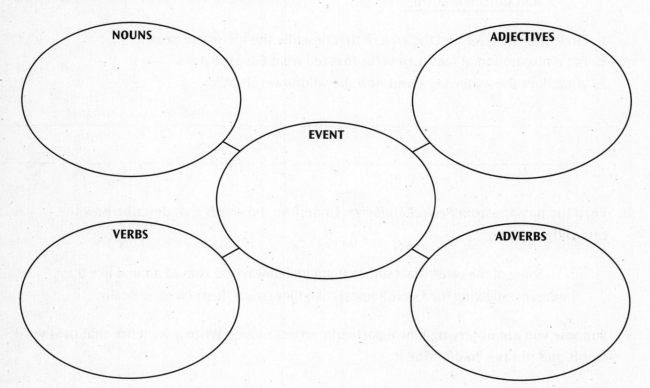

NOUNS

ADJECTIVES

EVENT

VERBS

ADVERBS

B. Use the words and phrases from your web to draft a short suspense story. Write it on
another sheet of paper.

© Harcourt

Name _____

The Parts of a Suspense Story

A **suspense story** is a tale in which a feeling of anticipation—or suspense—increases as a mystery unfolds. Here is an example of a suspense story written by a fifth grader. As you read it, think about how the student organized it. Then answer the questions.

Student Model

DRAFT

A Clatter in the Night
by Anna

Tina anxiously lay awake in her sleeping bag. There! She heard the mysterious clatter again! The noise came from the far end of the campsite and was getting closer. She thought it was most likely a raccoon or maybe a skunk.

Her brother George had heard it, too. A quiver in his voice told her he was petrified. "It's—" he barely whispered, "it's coming to eat us."

They had heard the sound the night before, and all day George had worked himself into a panic. He convinced himself that a horrible monster was sneaking though the woods.

Tina went out of the tent. She shivered in the darkness, and discovered that she too was a little scared. "What if it *is* a monster," she thought.

> **Introduce** the story. Identify the setting, characters, and conflict.

> **Develop** the ideas. Add vivid words and phrases that create a feeling of suspense.

> Use **adjectives and articles** to give details.

> **Organize** the plot. Describe the conflict in a way that makes the feeling of suspense grow.

> **Conclude** when the feeling of suspense is greatest.

1. Which sentence introduces the conflict of the story? Underline it.
2. Which part of the fourth sentence increases the feeling of suspense? Circle it.
3. Which sentence seems to take away from the feeling of suspense? Draw a line through it.
4. How do you know that George is scared by the sound? Use examples from the text.

_____

_____

_____

Name _____

Evaluate a Suspense Story

When you evaluate a suspense story, ask yourself how well the writer made the characters and events come alive. Also ask how well the writer used vivid words and phrases to help you share the feeling of anticipation and suspense.

Now evaluate the Student Model. Put a check beside each thing the writer did well. If you do not think the writer did a good job, do not check the box.

☐ The writer introduced the story by identifying the setting, characters, and conflict.

☐ The writer developed the ideas by adding vivid words that help create a feeling of suspense.

☐ The writer organized the plot to make the feeling of suspense grow.

☐ The writer concluded the story when the feeling of suspense was greatest.

Writer's Grammar
Adjectives and Articles

An **adjective** is a word that describes a noun or pronoun. An adjective can tell *what kind, how many,* or *which one*.

Example   **ancient** scroll   **two** eggs   **cracked** window

The adjectives *a, an,* and *the* are called **articles**. *The* refers to a specific person, place, thing, or idea. *A* is used before a noun that begins with a consonant sound. *An* is used before a noun that begins with a vowel sound.

Example   **the** oldest detective   **a** scroll   **an** egg

Read the sentences. Circle the articles. Underline the other adjectives.

1. A suspicious package was left on the porch.
2. The wooden steps creaked as I walked up them.
3. Renee saw an ugly crack in the stone wall.
4. Terrence walked into the empty room.

© Harcourt

Name _____

Revise: Adding Vivid Words and Phrases

One thing the writer could have done better was to use vivid words and phrases. These would have helped develop the feeling of suspense. She could have done this by asking *who, what, where, when, why,* and *how*. Here is an example of how a sentence from the Student Model could be improved.

Example   **Read:** Tina went out of the tent.

Ask Yourself: *How* did she go out of the tent?

Ask Yourself: *What* did she feel *when* she was going outside?

Improve the Sentence: *Tina nervously crept out of the tent.*

A. Read the following sentences. Then improve them by adding vivid words and phrases and by using adjectives to add details. Use the Word Bank to help you.

1. John went into the room and told his brother to do something.

   _____

   _____

2. Helena opened the door and saw the box.

   _____

   _____

3. Mr. Phelps filled the hole in the lawn.

   _____

   _____

4. The little cat walked across the room.

   _____

   _____

Word Bank

ancient
closet
confidently
demand
discover
edge
fresh
carefully
living room
open
silently

B. Revise the draft of a suspense story that you wrote on page 112. Be sure that you have used vivid words and phrases to bring the characters and events to life. Write your revision on another sheet of paper.

© Harcourt

Name _____

Review Writer's Craft

In this unit you have learned how sensory details can be used to make writing come alive for readers. You have also learned how to use vivid words and phrases to make writing more lively and more entertaining.

A. Read the following passage. Notice how the writer used sensory details and vivid words and phrases.

Literature Model

(1) Telegraph wires reached from coast to coast by this time. (2) Invented by Samuel Morse in 1837, the telegraph was a sort of electric switch. (3) Current passing through it could be turned on and off with the tap of a finger. (4) Messages were created by sending long or short pulses of current through a telegraph at one end of a wire to another telegraph at the other end of the wire. (5) At the receiving end of the wire, marks were indented on a roll of paper tape moving around a cylinder, a device called a Morse register. (6) Long pulses made dashes, short pulses made dots. (7) Morse created a code in which the dots and dashes represented the letters of the alphabet. (8) Telegraph operators receiving a message translated the code into letters and wrote them down.

—from *Inventing the Future: A Photobiography of Thomas Alva Edison*
by Marfé Ferguson Delano

B. Identify how the writer used sensory details.
   1. Underline the words in the third sentence that appeal to the sense of touch.
   2. Circle the specific nouns used in the sixth sentence.

C. Write two sentences that describe how the telegraph works. Use sensory details and vivid words and phrases to make your description come alive.

_____

_____

_____

_____

Name _____

A Closer Look at Writer's Craft

Review Writer's Craft

The traits of **voice** and **word choice** can make your writing more lively and more interesting.

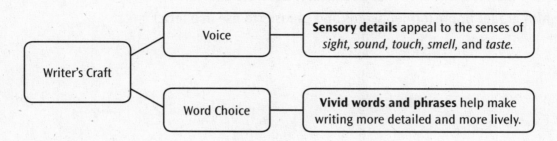

A. Read each sentence. Underline the sensory details that appeal to the sense mentioned in parentheses.

Example Its horn <u>bellowed</u> <u>loudly</u> as the truck <u>roared</u> down the road. (sound)

1. Amanda buried her bare feet in the cool, wet sand. (touch)
2. My grandfather prefers fruit juice that is not too sweet and not too bitter. (taste)
3. The dry branches and leaves crackled and popped in the campfire. (sound)
4. The chemicals from the science experiment made our noses twitch with a sharp, acidic odor. (smell)
5. A thick fog erased our view of the mountain. (sight)

B. Read the following passage from *Inventing the Future: A Photobiography of Thomas Alva Edison.*

> Next to the family's house, he built a 100-foot-high wooden tower, which he promoted as a tourist attraction. Anyone willing to pay 25 cents could climb to its top and enjoy a bird's-eye view of the lake and surrounding countryside.

1. Underline two verbs in the first sentence that describe a specific action.
2. Circle two vivid phrases in the first sentence that describe the tower.
3. Write a sentence describing what tourists might see from the top of the tower. Use details from the passage.

_____

_____

Writer's Companion • UNIT 4
Lesson 19 *Review Writer's Craft*

Name _____

Review Writer's Craft

In a **letter of request**, the writer asks for information, orders something, or asks a person or organization to do something. Sensory details and vivid words and phrases can help writers make sure that a request is accurate and clear. Here is how one fifth grader brainstormed words and phrases to use in a letter of request.

Example

Subject: *Playground*

To: *Principal Chen*

Request: *Plant some trees and grass in the school playground.*

Sensory Details I Can Use				
Sight	**Sound**	**Touch**	**Smell**	**Taste**
shade		*sweltering*	*pine*	
trees		*heat*		

Vivid Words I Can Use
propose
welcomed

Vivid Phrases I Can Use
like stepping onto hot coals

A. Use the information in the chart to answer these questions.

1. What request does the writer make?

_____

2. What words does the writer plan on using to appeal to the sense of touch?

_____

B. Use the chart to write a sentence that tells why the writer wants the school to plant some trees.

_____

_____

_____

© Harcourt

Name _____

The Parts of a Letter of Request

In a **letter of request**, the writer asks for information or for someone to do something. Sensory details and vivid words and phrases can make sure that the request is understood. Here is an example of a letter of request written by a fifth grader. As you read it, think about how the student organized it. Then answer the questions.

Student Model

DRAFT

Dear Principal Chen,

I am writing to request that the school create a "green area."

Right now, the playground is covered with concrete and black rubber mats that absorb heat like a sponge absorbs water. There is no escape from the sweltering heat of the midday sun. Stepping onto the playground on a hot day is like stepping onto hot coals.

I propose that the school plant some trees, bushes, and grass. Think of how cool it would be. I am sure the natural beauty of a "green area" would be a welcomed sight to both the students and teachers. Thank you for your attention.

Sincerely,

April Anderson

Write a return address and an inside address. Follow the correct style and spell names correctly.

Greet the person by name.

Organize the body of the letter by first describing your request.

Develop your request with sensory details and vivid words and phrases.

Conclude by summing up your request.

End your letter with a "thank you" and a **closing** such as *Sincerely* or *Yours truly*. Then sign it.

Address an envelope.

1. Find the greeting and the closing of the letter. Underline them.
2. Which sentence introduces the writer's request? Circle it.
3. Which vivid phrase in the second paragraph describes what covers the playground now? Put a box around it.
4. Rewrite the sentence, "Think of how cool it would be." Add vivid words that help develop the request.

_____

_____

Evaluate a Letter of Request

A. Two students were asked to write a letter of request about improving their community. The letter below received a score of 4. When using a 4-point rubric, a score of 4 means "excellent." Read the letter and the comments to find out why it is a success.

Student Model

Dear Mayor Penn,

    I am writing to request permission for my art class to restore the mural on the back wall of the fire station on Union Street. As you probably know, the mural is dedicated to the diverse groups of people who give to our community.

    Over the years, the colors of the mural have faded, and layers of paint are peeling off in large pieces. It is a shame to think that as the colors of the mural fade, so might our memories. We need to respect the people who have made our community a safe place to live, learn, work, and grow.

    With the city's permission, my art class will restore the mural to its original condition. We will scrub the wall ourselves and then add new, bright layers of paint to bring out the way it used to look.

    When we finish, the people who see the mural will think they can actually hear the hammering of the workers painted on the wall. They will think they can actually smell the fresh-baked bread floating from the bakery. They will think they have actually seen the bravery of the firefighters.

    If the city grants us permission to renovate the mural, the community will be thankful.

                      Sincerely,

                      Hector Rosa

> Good. You greet the person by name.

> Nice work. You clearly describe the request that you are making.

> Nice! You use vivid words and phrases to show why your request is important.

> Good. You use all types of pronouns correctly.

> Well done! You use vivid and sensory details to describe the impact the renovation will have.

> Good. You use an appropriate ending and closing for your letter.

© Harcourt

Name _____

B. This letter received a score of 2. Why did it get a low score?

Student Model

Dear Mr. Pearson,

Our town should start having a festival every summer.

The festival could be held in Forrest Park. It could feature concerts, art shows, and tasty local food. It would be a good way for many people to expose theirselves to all the good things that the community has to offer. Everybody likes festivals.

The festival could also help the city to make some extra money that it could spend on music and arts.

Sincerely,

Mary Rosetti

> Good. You use a proper greeting and closing.

> You state what you are requesting, but you need to describe your request more completely.

> Good. You use vivid words like *tasty* and *expose*. But you should use more of them. They will make your request more convincing.

> Be sure that you use the correct form of reflexive case pronouns. The correct form is *themselves*.

C. What score would you give the student's story? Put a number on each line.

	4	3	2	1
Voice _____	☐ The writer uses many sensory details.	☐ The writer uses some sensory details.	☐ The writer uses few sensory details.	☐ The writer uses no sensory details.
Word Choice _____	☐ The writer uses many vivid words and phrases.	☐ The writer uses some vivid words and phrases.	☐ The writer uses few vivid words or phrases.	☐ The writer uses no vivid words or phrases.
Conventions _____	☐ The writer uses all pronouns and adjectives correctly.	☐ The writer sometimes uses pronouns and adjectives correctly.	☐ The writer rarely uses pronouns and adjectives correctly.	☐ The writer does not use any pronouns or adjectives correctly.

Name _____

Extended Writing/Test Prep

On the first two pages of this lesson, you will use what you have learned about
voice and word choice to write a longer written work.

A. **Read the three choices below. Put a star by the writing activity you would like to do.**

1. Respond to a Writing Prompt

   Writing Situation: Sometimes communities can do things that help make life better
   for everyone.

   Directions for Writing: Think of something your community could do to make life better for
   its residents. Write a letter of request to your community leaders. Use sensory details and
   vivid words to help explain your request. Be sure to use a return address, an inside address,
   a greeting, a body, and a closing.

2. Choose one of the pieces of writing you started in this unit:

   - a narrative paragraph (page 100)

   - a skit (page 106)

   - a suspense story (page 112)

   Revise and expand your draft into a complete piece of writing. Use what you have learned
   about voice and word choice.

3. Choose a topic you would like to write about. You may write a narrative paragraph,
   a skit, a suspense story, or a letter of request. Use sensory details and vivid words and
   phrases. Be sure to create specific voices for different characters.

B. **Use the space below and on the next page to plan your writing.**

TOPIC: _____

WRITING FORM: _____

HOW WILL I ORGANIZE MY WRITING: _____

_____

_____

_____

© Harcourt

Name _____

C. In the space below, draw a graphic organizer that will help you plan
your writing. Fill in the graphic organizer. Write additional notes on
the lines below.

Notes

_____

_____

_____

_____

_____

_____

_____

D. Do your writing on another sheet of paper.

Answering Multiple-Choice Questions

For questions on pages 124–127, fill in the bubble next to the correct answer.

A. Gabriella made the chart below to organize ideas for a paper. Use her chart to answer questions 1–3.

Gabriella's Writing Plan

Setting: art museum

Name of Character	Detective Rita Gomez
Personality	• very serious • nice, but rarely smiles • never raises her voice
Words that Character Might Use	• interesting • evidence • I presume

1. Which personality trait fits the character and should be added to the chart?
   (A) She often yells at people.
   (B) She is always joking around with her friends.
   (C) She quietly and calmly does her job.
   (D) She isn't very nice to people she doesn't know.

2. Which word or phrase does not fit the character's voice and should not be added to the chart?
   (A) "I hate that!"
   (B) "Be careful when you move that."
   (C) "Let's think about the facts."
   (D) "May I look at that package, please?"

3. Based on the information in Gabriella's Writing Plan, what kind of paper is Gabriella planning to write?
   (A) a newspaper story about the art museum
   (B) a paper that tells a story about Detective Gomez
   (C) a paper that tells the story of Gabriella's life
   (D) a letter of request to Detective Gomez

Test Tip:
A character's voice is the unique way that he or she speaks. For Question 2, choose the word or phrase that sounds most different from those in the chart.

© Harcourt

Name _____

B. The story below is a first draft that Billy wrote. The story contains
mistakes. Read the story to answer questions 1–3.

Buried Treasure

(1) The metal detector made a noise. (2) "Something is down there,"
Tim said. (3) "Naw, it's probably just a stinky old steel pipe," said Jake.
(4) Tim started digging. (5) He hoped it was a chest of gold coins like in
the pirate movies. (6) As he dug, he thought about all the things he could
buy with the gold. (7) On his last dig into the dirt, the shovel hit something.
(8) Tim got down and looked. (9) He pulled the jar out and scraped off the
dirt. (10) "What's in it?" Jake asked. (11) "Coins," Tim said. (12) He held the
jar up to the light, so they both could see. (13) "Pennies!" they said.

1. Which sentence contains dialogue that best creates a specific voice
   for one of the characters?

   (A) sentence (2)

   (B) sentence (3)

   (C) sentence (11)

   (D) sentence (13)

2. Which sentence below could be added after sentence (7) to give
   a more vivid description of the events in the paragraph?

   (A) His pants were already dirty.

   (B) Jake shuffled his feet in the dirt and waited.

   (C) His glasses slid to the end of his nose.

   (D) He saw a jar, sunken in the dirt and protected by flat stones.

> **Test Tip:**
> A sensory detail
> appeals to the senses
> of *sight, sound, taste,
> touch,* or *smell.*
> For Question 3,
> choose the sentence
> that uses these
> types of details most
> effectively.

3. Which sentence below best shows how sentence (8) could be
   revised to give sensory details?

   (A) Tim walked around and looked.

   (B) Tim examined things closely and carefully.

   (C) Tim knelt in the damp hole and brushed away clumps of soil.

   (D) Tim thought about what could be there.

© Harcourt

Writer's Companion • UNIT 4
Lesson 20 *Writing Test Practice*

C. Read the story, "The Search." Choose the word or words that correctly complete questions 1–5.

The Search

Mr. Franks and I set off on ____(1)____ mission to find ____(2)____ ruins of the mining camp. I brought extra water for ____(3)____, because I knew it was going to be an especially hot and humid day. As we walked deeper into the woods, ____(4)____ pushed through the thick vines. Mr. Franks was only five feet ahead of me, but I could barely see ____(5)____! The briers stuck to our pants, as if to hold us back from discovering the secret they hid. Finally, after two hours, I stumbled over a clue that we were close—a rusty wheel of a coal car!

1. Which answer should go in blank (1)?
   - (A) we
   - (B) our
   - (C) ours

2. Which answer should go in blank (2)?
   - (A) the
   - (B) a
   - (C) an

3. Which answer should go in blank (3)?
   - (A) me
   - (B) mine
   - (C) myself

4. Which answer should go in blank (4)?
   - (A) we
   - (B) us
   - (C) ourselves

5. Which answer should go in blank (5)?
   - (A) he
   - (B) himself
   - (C) him

> **Test Tip:**
>
> A pronoun that comes after an action verb or preposition is an object pronoun.
>
> Singular object pronouns: *me, you, him, her, it*
>
> Plural object pronouns: *us, you, them*

© Harcourt

Name _____

D. Read and answer questions 1–3.

1. Put the ideas in the box together to create a sentence that makes sense.

saw the
famous
she
painting

   Which sentence correctly combines the words from the box?

   (A) She saw the famous painting.

   (B) She saw the painting famous.

   (C) She famous saw the painting.

2. Put the ideas in the box together to create a sentence that makes sense.

apple fell from
tree
an
the

   Which sentence correctly combines the words from the box?

   (A) The apple fell from an tree.

   (B) An apple fell from the tree.

   (C) The tree an apple fell from.

   Test Tip:

   The adjectives *a, an,* and *the* are called articles. Use *a* before a consonant sound, and use *an* before a vowel sound.

3. Put the ideas in the box together to create a sentence that makes sense.

herself
she
to talk to
told
them

   Which sentence correctly combines the words from the box?

   (A) Them told she to talk to herself.

   (B) She told them to talk to herself.

   (C) She told herself to talk to them.

Name _____

Identify: Sentences with Facts and Reasons

When they write to persuade, writers voice their opinions. They develop and support their opinions by writing sentences with facts and reasons. **Facts** are statements that can be proven. **Reasons** are statements that explain why readers should agree with the writer.

A. Read the following passage from *Interrupted Journey: Saving Endangered Sea Turtles*. Pay attention to the facts and reasons the writer gives to support her opinion.

Literature Model

Max and his mother and the other volunteers work for a vital cause. All sea turtles are threatened or endangered; Kemp's ridleys are the most endangered of all. Right now on our planet there are fewer than eight thousand Kemp's ridley turtles left. They are a vanishing species.

—from *Interrupted Journey: Saving Endangered Sea Turtles*
by Kathryn Lasky

B. Identify opinions, facts, and reasons in the passage.
1. Underline the phrase in the first sentence that shows an opinion.
2. Draw a box around a reason that supports this opinion.
3. Circle a statement that is a fact and can be proven.

C. In your own words, summarize the passage. Tell the writer's opinion and the reasons and facts she gives for her opinion.

_____

_____

_____

_____

Name _____

Explore: Sentences with Facts and Reasons

Opinions are a matter of personal belief. They cannot be proven right or wrong.
When you write to persuade someone of your opinion, you must use **facts** and
reasons to support your point of view.

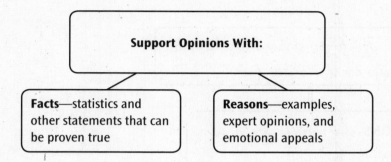

Support Opinions With:

Facts—statistics and other statements that can be proven true

Reasons—examples, expert opinions, and emotional appeals

A. **Read each sentence. Tell whether the sentence states a fact, reason, or opinion.**

> **Example**   *A Tree Grows in Brooklyn* is a wonderful book. *opinion* _____

1. Betty Smith's first novel, *A Tree Grows in Brooklyn*, is considered an American classic.

   _____

2. The book sold 300,000 copies in the first six weeks after it was published.

   _____

3. The main character, Francie, is more interesting than any other character in the book.

   _____

B. **Read these sentences from *Interrupted Journey: Saving Endangered Sea Turtles*. Then underline the words that tell facts and draw boxes around the words that tell reasons.**

> Richie Moretti is the owner, director, and founder of the hospital. He is not
> a veterinarian. He is not a marine biologist. He is a man who loves turtles, and
> his calling in life is to help injured animals.

C. **Write a sentence with an opinion that could be supported by the facts and reasons above.**

_____

_____

© Harcourt

Name _____

Use: Sentences with Facts and Reasons

In a **persuasive letter**, the writer presents an opinion about a problem and suggests an action that should be taken. Before you write, you will want to organize your ideas and information. Here is how one student started to organize her persuasive letter.

Example

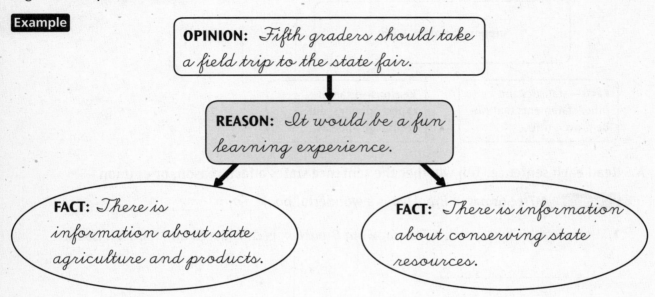

OPINION: *Fifth graders should take a field trip to the state fair.*

REASON: *It would be a fun learning experience.*

FACT: *There is information about state agriculture and products.*

FACT: *There is information about conserving state resources.*

A. Think about a place you would like your class to go on a field trip. Write a sentence that states your opinion. Then complete the graphic organizer.

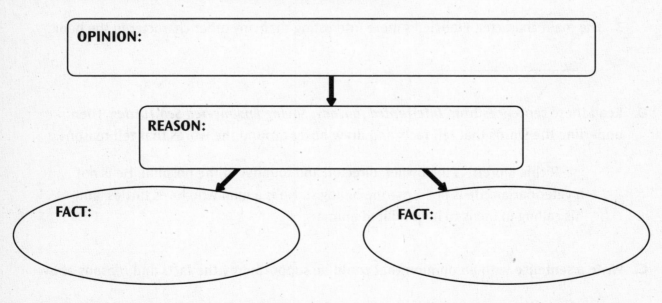

OPINION:

REASON:

FACT:

FACT:

B. Use information from the graphic organizer to draft a persuasive letter to your teacher or principal. Write it on another sheet of paper.

© Harcourt

Name _____

The Parts of a Persuasive Letter

A good **persuasive letter** offers an opinion and convinces readers that the opinion is correct. Here is a draft of a persuasive letter written by a fifth grader. As you read it, think about how the student organized her opinions, facts, and reasons. Then answer the questions.

Student Model

DRAFT

Dear Principal Sahi,

    I am writing to request that the fifth grade be taken on a field trip to the state fair. The fair is a unique opportunity to see real-life examples of things we have learned about in school. Plus, it would be so much fun! Fifth graders learned about agriculture this year. Many of the fair's exhibits feature agricultural products produced in our state. Conserving natural resources is another topic we have studied recently. Some of the exhibits inform fairgoers of what is being done to preserve our farmland.

    "Why do I need to learn this?" is a question you often hear from students. Here is the perfect chance to show students the practical reasons for what they learn. Please, won't you consider taking advantage of this educational opportunity?

                      Sincerely,

                      Keisha Clemmons

Greet the person by name. Be sure to check your spelling.

Organize the letter by politely stating your opinion and the reasons and facts that support your opinion.

Finish the body of your letter with a call to action.

End your letter with an appropriate closing. Sign your name.

1. Which sentence states the purpose of the letter? Underline it.
2. Find two facts or reasons the writer gives to support her opinion. Write them below.

_____

_____

3. Is the sentence "Plus, it would be so much fun!" a good supporting sentence? Why or why not?

_____

_____

Name _____

Evaluate a Persuasive Letter

When you evaluate a persuasive letter, ask yourself if the writer's opinions, facts, and reasons are convincing.

Now evaluate the Student Model. Put a check in the box next to each thing the writer did well. If you do not think the writer did a good job, do not check the box.

☐ The writer wrote a greeting.
☐ The writer stated her opinion clearly and politely.
☐ The writer organized the letter by stating an opinion and giving facts and reasons to support it.
☐ The writer used persuasive details.
☐ The writer concluded with a call to action and signed the letter.

Writer's Grammar
Action and Linking Verbs

Action verbs describe an action. The action may be physical or mental. *Jump* and *consider* are examples of action verbs.

Linking verbs do not describe an action. They link, or connect, a noun or pronoun with another word. The verb *to be* is often used as a linking verb. *Are* and *seem* are examples of linking verbs.

Underline the verb in each sentence. Then write *action* or *linking* to tell what kind of verb it is.

1. The telephone is on the table in the hall.   _____

2. Eric felt upset yesterday after school.   _____

3. They hurry to the park for a game of baseball.   _____

4. I ran up the stairs with the letter in my hand.   _____

5. Zora asked Juliet the question.   _____

6. Enrique and Elvia are from Venezuela.   _____

© Harcourt

Name _____

Revise: Adding Persuasive Details

One thing the writer might have done better is to use more persuasive details—facts or reasons—to support her opinion. Here is how a sentence from the Student Model can be improved.

Example Fifth graders learned about agriculture this year.

This year, fifth graders had an entire social studies unit focused on state agriculture.

A. Revise these sentences by adding persuasive details. Remember that details can be facts or reasons. You can use the Word Bank to help you.

1. A lot of kids think there is no reason to learn math.

_____

_____

_____

2. There are a lot of neat exhibits at the state fair.

_____

_____

3. People say the fair is a chance to celebrate.

_____

_____

_____

> **Word Bank**
>
> classroom
>
> director
>
> educational
>
> history
>
> pride
>
> skills

B. Revise the draft you wrote on page 130. Add persuasive details that support your opinion. Write your letter on another sheet of paper.

© Harcourt

Name _____

Identify: Varying Sentence Type and Length

A good way to write effectively is to vary the type and length of the sentences you write. You can have questions, statements, commands, and exclamations. You can write simple and compound sentences as well as sentences that contain items in a series. You can also combine short, choppy sentences into longer sentences that are smoother and easier to read.

A. Read the following passage from *The Power of W.O.W!*. Notice how the writer uses a variety of sentence types and lengths.

Literature Model

Mrs. Nguyen: (Sighs, and her shoulders slump) Words on Wheels won't be back after next week.

Ileana: Why not?

Mrs. Nguyen: Words on Wheels is just a pilot program. The library funded W.O.W. for one year, and the year's almost up. There's no more money to pay for gas and repairs, to pay the driver, or to buy new books. I'll have to go back to the library downtown.

—from *The Power of W.O.W!*
by Crystal Hubbard

B. Identify the examples of sentence variety in the passage.
1. Underline the compound sentence.
2. Draw boxes around two simple sentences.
3. Circle the sentence that lists items in a series.

C. Rewrite the last sentence in the passage as a question.

_____

_____

_____

_____

© Harcourt

Name _____

Explore: Varying Sentence Type and Length

Varying sentence type and length is a great way to make sentences more enjoyable for readers. You can also emphasize information this way. When you write, review your sentences. Consider how you might change your sentences in length or form to make the writing both interesting and clear.

```
┌──────────────────────────────┐
│   Strategies for Variation   │
└──────────────────────────────┘
```

Vary sentence type.
- Write simple and compound sentences.
- Write sentences with items in a series.
- Write statements, questions, commands, and exclamations.

Vary sentence length.
- Alternate short and long sentences.
- Combine short sentences into longer sentences.

A. Write a new sentence that includes the information from each item below. You can use any strategy to change the sentence.

Example Al went to the store and bought some peanuts.

Did Al buy some peanuts when he went to the store?

1. I ran all the way home. I did my homework in a flash.

_____

_____

2. We caught eleven fireflies last night. Then we let them go.

_____

_____

3. Jorge speaks French. He also speaks some Spanish and Portuguese.

_____

_____

B. Read these sentences from *The Power of W.O.W.!*. Underline the compound sentence.

Ileana: I wish I had King Midas's golden touch. I could turn this picnic table into gold, and then we could sell it to pay for W.O.W..

Name _____

Use: Varying Sentence Type and Length

In a **persuasive paragraph**, the writer's purpose is to convince readers to believe, or act, in a certain way. Before you write to persuade, you will want to think about how to include persuasive language and sentence variety in your paragraph. Here is how one student started to organize a paragraph about her favorite city.

Example

My Opinion	Facts and Reasons	Persuasive Language	Ways to Vary Sentences
Boulder, Colorado, is a great place to live.	Rocky Mountains Arts and cultural activities Won awards	Natural beauty Special place	Combine short, choppy sentences. Write simple and compound sentences.

A. What is a place you think is special? Think about how you would persuade someone of your opinion. Then complete the graphic organizer.

My Opinion	Facts and Reasons	Persuasive Language	Ways to Vary Sentences

B. Use information from the graphic organizer to draft a paragraph that would persuade people to agree with you. Make sure that you create sentence variety by using different types and lengths of sentences. Write it on another sheet of paper.

© Harcourt

Name _____

The Parts of a Persuasive Paragraph

An effective **persuasive paragraph** begins with a strong opinion statement and uses facts, examples, or personal experiences to support that statement. Here is a first draft of a persuasive paragraph written by a fifth grader. As you read it, think about how the student organized the paragraph. Then answer the questions.

Student Model

**Boulder: A Superior City
by Cristina**

Boulder, Colorado, is a truly special place. There are many wonderful things to do and see in this great city. You can go hiking in Chautauqua Park. You can go sledding in Scott Carpenter Park. You can visit Boulder's art museums, libraries, and cultural festivals, too. My family has gone to the Annual Colorado Cowboy Poetry Gathering three times, and it's more fun each time we go. Boulder has more than just recreation. In Boulder, the natural beauty of the Rocky Mountains greets you each day. And the city's transportation and senior services are first-rate. It's no wonder Boulder was named "Best All Around Dream Town." No matter who you are or what you enjoy, Boulder is the place for you—guaranteed!

Introduce your opinion in a clear topic sentence.

Organize your paragraph by naming reasons and details that support your opinion.

Use a variety of sentence types and lengths.

Conclude with a strong sentence that restates your opinion.

1. Which sentence states the writer's opinion? Underline it.
2. Write an example of each type of sentence.

Simple: _____

Compound: _____

_____

3. What is the writer's purpose in this paragraph? Who do you think the intended audience is?

_____

_____

Name _____

Evaluate a Persuasive Paragraph

When you evaluate a persuasive paragraph, ask yourself if the writer stated an opinion clearly and used facts and reasons to support it. You should also ask whether the writer used sentence variety to keep the writing from becoming repetitive.

Now evaluate the Student Model. Put a check in the box next to each thing the writer did well. If you do not think the writer did a good job, do not check the box.

- ☐ The writer stated an opinion in a clear topic sentence.
- ☐ The writer included reasons and details to support the opinion.
- ☐ The writer used persuasive language.
- ☐ The writer used a variety of sentence types and lengths.
- ☐ The writer concluded with a strong restatement of her opinion.

Writer's Grammar
Present Tense; Subject-Verb Agreement

Verbs in the **present tense** describe actions that are happening now. They end in *–s* or *–es* or have no ending, depending upon whose action they are expressing.

When you write, pay attention to **subject-verb agreement.** Singular subjects should have singular verbs, and plural subjects should have plural verbs.

Singular	Plural
I sing	we sing
you sing	you sing
she/he sings	they sing

Complete each sentence. Write the correct present-tense form of the verb in parentheses.

1. The traffic light _____ from red to green every two minutes. (to change)

2. The children _____ late to the party. (to arrive)

3. In the springtime, bees _____ flowers. (to pollinate)

4. He _____ both karate and jujitsu. (to study)

© Harcourt

Name _____

Revise: Varying Sentences

One thing the writer could have done better is to use more variety in her sentences. Here is how two sentences from the Student Model can be combined so there is not so much repetition.

Example You can go hiking in Chautauqua Park. You can go sledding in Scott Carpenter Park.

You can go hiking in Chautauqua Park and sledding in Scott Carpenter Park.

A. Revise these sentences by combining them or changing sentence type or length in some other way.

1. I realized I was hungry. I realized I had an apple in my backpack.

_____

_____

2. They have really good books at our library. They also have lectures and films.

_____

_____

3. I saw deer on my hike in the woods. I saw a moose, too.

_____

_____

4. We know you'll love Washington, D.C. Washington, D.C., is the nation's capital.

_____

_____

B. Revise the draft you wrote on page 136. Improve sentences by varying sentence type and length. Write your revision on another sheet of paper.

© Harcourt

Name _____

Identify: Create a Memorable Ending

The final part of a piece of writing is called the **ending**. Endings can have different purposes. An ending may sum up information, call for action, suggest an emotion, or restate a theme. Whatever the purpose of the ending, creating an ending that is **memorable** means creating an ending that is interesting, meaningful, or unusual enough that readers will not forget it.

A. Read the final paragraph from *Any Small Goodness: A Novel of the Barrio.* Notice how the writer sums up what has happened in the story and delivers a message to readers.

Literature Model

Now Huitla's home. Sleeping on the sofa in a happy sprawl of fur. I sit beside her, totally sunken down. Our sofa's so soft, sitting on it's like being swallowed by a clam. I think about old Leo Love, who Abuelita now calls *El Estimado,* The Esteemed One. Going against allergies and dizziness and possible broken bones to save our cat.

You could do worse than be like such a person.

—from *Any Small Goodness: A Novel of the Barrio*
by Tony Johnston

B. Identify how the writer creates a memorable ending.
1. Underline the sentences that tell where the narrator's missing cat is now.
2. Draw a box around a sentence that tells who the narrator is thinking about.
3. Circle the sentence that delivers the writer's personal message.

C. The writer's final sentence is an understatement. An understatement is a statement that is less powerful than you might expect. What is another way the writer might have written the final sentence?

_____

_____

© Harcourt

Name _____

Explore: Create a Memorable Ending

The ending of a poem, essay, or book is the last thing readers see. Hopefully, the words the writer uses for it will stay with readers for a long time. When you write an ending, think about the lasting impression you wish to make and choose your words carefully.

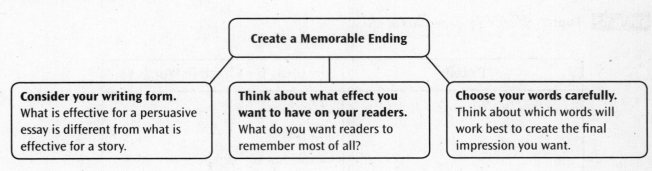

Create a Memorable Ending

Consider your writing form.
What is effective for a persuasive essay is different from what is effective for a story.

Think about what effect you want to have on your readers.
What do you want readers to remember most of all?

Choose your words carefully.
Think about which words will work best to create the final impression you want.

A. Match each sentence to the purpose the sentence would serve as an ending to a piece of writing.

> Example

___B___ Come to our rally at Smith Street this Saturday to show your support!

A. Deliver a message to the reader.

1. _____ But she didn't need to be praised—she was so proud to have finally conquered her fear.

B. Invite the reader to take action.

2. _____ It's always good to be reminded that you can't judge a book by its cover.

C. Resolve a character's problem.

B. Read the paragraph. Then write a final sentence for the ending.

My friend James is paralyzed from the waist down, so he uses a wheelchair. Daily tasks are sometimes very hard for him. But when he decided he wanted to play basketball, he didn't let anything stop him. He practiced many long hours before he could dribble and shoot with success. Now he plays in a local basketball league!

_____

_____

Name _____

Use: Create a Memorable Ending

In a short piece of writing, like a **poem**, every word counts. Before you write a poem, you will want to think about how you can use language most effectively—especially to create a memorable ending. Here is how one student started to think about word choice before writing a poem.

Example　**Topic:** *Watching a Butterfly*

Details	Ideas for Effective Words
Butterfly flying	*Flutters* *Dances* *Beating wings*
Sky above	*Milky blue*

A. Think about an animal you might choose as the topic for a poem. Write the name of the animal on the line. Then complete the chart

　　　Topic: _____

Details	Ideas for Effective Words

B. Use your completed chart to help you write a draft of a rhymed poem. Write your poem on another sheet of paper.

© Harcourt

Name _____

The Parts of a Poem

A **poem** is a piece of writing that is divided into lines and sometimes into groups of lines called stanzas. Here is a first draft of a poem written by a fifth grader. As you read it, think about how the student organized it. Then answer the questions.

Student Model

DRAFT

Butterfly Song
by Amity

As I lay quiet on the grass
Thinking about this day and last
Into the sky of milky blue
A brilliant yellow came into view.

As I watched the insect dance
Its flutter put me in a trance.
And in the beat of tiny wings
I heard just how a butterfly sings.

As I listened to its song
I learned the tune, and hummed along.
And we made music, the bug and I,
until it beat its wings goodbye.

Identify your topic in the title. You can also state it in a line of the poem.

Include sensory details and figurative language.

Develop a rhythm with your words. TIP: In a four-line stanza, you have a choice of rhyme schemes: *aabb*, *abab*, or *abcb*.

Create a memorable ending with a powerful image, metaphor, or simile.

1. What experience is the writer describing?

   _____

   _____

2. Which words help create mental images for you? Circle them.
3. What does the writer compare the butterfly's flight to?

   _____

   _____

Name _____

Evaluate a Poem

When you evaluate a poem, ask yourself if the writer introduced a focus and used figurative language and sensory details to develop it. You should also ask whether the writer created a memorable ending.

Now evaluate the Student Model. Put a check in the box next to each thing the writer did well. If you do not think the writer did a good job, do not check the box.

☐ The writer identified the focus of the poem.
☐ The writer included sensory details and figurative language.
☐ There is a clear rhythm in the poem.
☐ The writer created a memorable ending.

Writer's Grammar
Past and Future Tenses

Verbs in the **past tense** describe actions that have already happened. Most past tense verbs end in –ed. Irregular verbs have special forms that must be memorized.

Verbs in the **future tense** describe what will happen in the future. Most future tense verbs are formed by using will and the simple form of the verb.

Present	Past	Future
I walk	I walked	I will walk
it plays	it played	it will play
they grow	they grew	they will grow

Complete the table. Write the correct form for each missing verb.

Present Tense	Past Tense	Future Tense
push		
		will know
	joked	
		will study
	thought	
grin		

Name _____

Revise: Creating a More Specific Ending

One thing the writer might have done better is to create a more specific ending, using more exact words. Here is how the last stanza from the Student Model can be made more specific.

Example As I listened to its song
I learned the tune, and hummed along.
And we made music, the bug and I,
until it beat its wings goodbye.

As I listened to its song

I learned the tune, and hummed along.

We made soft music, the bug and I,

until it strummed itself goodbye.

A. Read the following lines of poetry. Then revise them to create a more specific ending. Use the Word Bank to help you.

The wave lifted my boat so high
It almost reached the sky.
And just as I crashed back into the sea,
Another wave came to frighten me.

Word Bank
mocking
rise
stormy
tormenting

_____

_____

_____

_____

_____

_____

B. Revise the draft you wrote on page 142. Make each word count. Pay special attention to the ending. Use another sheet of paper.

Name _____

Review Writer's Craft

By concentrating on sentence fluency and organization, your writing can become clearer, easier to understand, and more memorable. Successful writers use facts and reasons to develop their ideas, and they vary sentence type and length to hold readers' interest. They also think about the purpose of their writing and write an ending that will be remembered by their audience.

A. Read the passage below. Notice how the writer includes facts and reasons in his narrative. Notice, also, that he uses a variety of sentence types and lengths.

Literature Model

And now Chester had another thrill. For there weren't only sycamore trees in the park. The cricket could smell birches, beeches, and maples—elms, oaks—almost as many kinds of trees as Connecticut itself had to offer. And there was the moon!—the crescent moon—reflected in a little lake. Sounds, too, rose up to him: the shooshing of leaves, the nighttime countryside whispering of insects and little animals, and—best of all—a brook that was arguing with itself, as it splashed over rocks. The miracle of Central Park, a sheltered wilderness in the midst of the city, pierced Chester Cricket's heart with joy.

—from *Chester Cricket's Pigeon Ride*
by George Selden

B. Review what makes this writing clear, easy to understand, and memorable.
1. Look for different sentence types and lengths. Underline a simple sentence. Draw a box around a sentence that lists items in a series.
2. What is one fact given in the passage?

_____

C. Write a sentence that gives a reason for Chester's happiness.

_____

_____

Name _____

Review Writer's Craft

Sentence fluency and **organization** help writers achieve their purpose when they write.

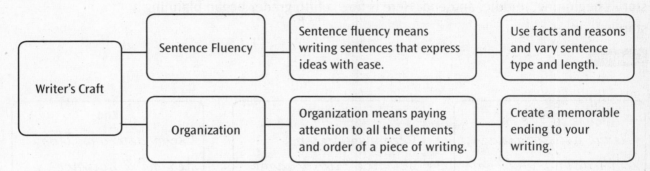

A. Read this passage from *Chester Cricket's Pigeon Ride*. Notice how the writer puts together sentence fluency and organization in the paragraph.

> What Chester had meant to say was that he was afraid he was suffering from a touch of acrophobia—fear of heights. (And perched on a pigeon's claw, on your way to the top of the Empire State, is not the best place to find that you are afraid of great heights.) But even if Lulu hadn't interrupted, the cricket couldn't have finished his sentence. His words were forced back into his throat. For the wind, which had been just a breeze beside the lake, was turning into a raging gale as they spiraled upward, around the building, floor past floor, and approached their final destination: the television antenna tower on the very top.

B. Change sentences in the passage.

1. Rewrite the first sentence as a question.

_____

_____

2. Rewrite the last sentence as three or more shorter sentences.

_____

_____

_____

_____

© Harcourt

Name _____

Review Writer's Craft

A **narrative composition** is a story. Some stories are fictional, or made up by writers. Before you write a story, you will want to plan what will happen in the story's beginning, middle, and end. Here is how a fifth grader began planning a story.

Example

Beginning	Middle	End
Clem, a fifth grader, isn't doing well on her science tests. "Why can't I get As?" she asks herself.	Clem creates a science trivia game to play with her friend Juan.	Clem gets an A on her next science test, and her teacher asks her to teach the game to the class.

A. Use the graphic organizer above to answer the questions below.

1. Who will be the main character of the story?

_____

2. What problem does Clem face?

_____

_____

3. How does Clem solve the problem?

_____

_____

4. How has the student already begun working on sentence variety?

_____

_____

Name _____

The Parts of a Narrative Composition

The basic elements of a **narrative composition** are the characters, setting, and plot. Here is an example of a story written by a fifth grader. As you read it, think about how the student organized the story. Then answer the questions.

Student Model

DRAFT

Score!
by Tia

Clem looked at the paper on her desk and felt miserable. She had bombed her science test, and it wasn't the first time. Why couldn't she get *A*s on everything, like her friend Juan?

After school, Clem met Juan on the soccer field for a game. Playing soccer was always fun. Suddenly, Clem had an idea. Maybe if she made studying a game, it wouldn't seem difficult or boring.

The next day, Juan and Clem used cardboard to make a game board and their science notes to write questions. Juan won the first two games, but Clem won the third. They played until Juan had to go home, and they played every day that week.

The next week, Clem smiled when Ms. Pérez handed back her science test with a big *A* written across the top. But better than the grade was Ms. Pérez's request—she wanted Clem to bring *Science Showdown* to school so the entire class could play!

Introduce the story by identifying the setting and characters.

Organize the plot by describing the problem and arranging the events in time order.

Use a variety of sentence types and lengths to keep readers' interest.

Conclude with an ending that is memorable. Resolve the problem and include a message if you think there should be one.

1. Which sentence introduces the main character and setting? Underline it.
2. What makes Clem think about making a game to help her study?

_____

_____

3. Do you think the ending works? Explain why or why not.

_____

_____

_____

Name _____

Evaluate a Narrative Composition

A. Two students were asked to write a narrative composition about a person who solves a problem creatively. The story below got a score of 4. When using a 4-point rubric, a score of 4 means "excellent." Read the story and the teacher comments that go with it. Find out why this story is a success.

Student Model

Homemade Holiday
by Nathan

Staring out the window, Zach frowned. More snow. Back in Florida, he'd imagined how much fun he'd have sledding once he moved to Maine. But snow kept falling heavy and thick. After three days, he still couldn't go outdoors—not even to take a walk.

> Good work! You introduced the main character and the setting in the beginning.

Zach sighed. In Florida he could play tag, go swimming, or ride his bike all year long. It was like every day was a holiday. "That's it!" thought Zach. "I'll invent a holiday, and it will be today."

> Great—You've introduced a problem and shown how it gets resolved.

Zach drew pictures of beaches and palm trees. He wrote *Florida in Maine Day* across the bottom, and hung them on the walls. He put on a swimsuit and sunglasses. Then he lay on his inflatable raft, and turned on the radio.

> Each event is told in order—perfect.

Just then Zach's mother came in, carrying a bowl of orange cubes. "Where did you get it, Mom?" he asked. But as soon as he took a bite, he knew. She'd frozen orange juice into cubes. Zach smiled. Florida in Maine Day just might be a pretty good holiday after all.

> Nice. You've made a point of varying sentence type and length.

> Your ending is terrific. Excellent work.

B. This narrative got a score of 2. Why did it get a low score?

Student Model

Designing a Dream
by Samuel

Jake loved climbing trees. He can sit for hours up in their leafy branches. He enjoys gazing at the forest around him.

One day, Jake decides he wants a tree house. He closed his eyes, and immediately saw the big, tall, sturdy oak tree down by the gurgling creek. It was the ideal place for Jake to build.

Jake and his dad worked hard to design the perfect tree house. Jake's dad constructed the ladder and climbed up into the oak tree. He soon discovered that there were many weak branches. It seemed the tree were not so sturdy, after all. Then Jake figured out how to build beams that would provide extra support. His tree house dream could finally become a reality!

> You've introduced the character, but the setting isn't clear. Can you show readers how Jake feels about trees rather than telling them?

> You've done a nice job using a variety of sentence types and lengths. Watch your subject-verb agreement and keep the tense consistent.

> You've introduced a problem and its resolution. But you waited until the end. You need to develop this part of the narrative more.

> How could you make your ending exciting or unusual?

C. What score would you give the student's story? Put a number on each line.

	4	3	2	1
Sentence Fluency _____	☐ There is a lot of variety in sentence type and length. There are many concrete details to develop ideas.	☐ There is some variety in sentence type and length. There are enough details to develop ideas.	☐ There is not much variety in sentence type and length. There are some details to develop ideas.	☐ Most sentences are of the same type and length. Ideas are not developed.
Organization _____	☐ There is a clear beginning, middle, and end. The ending is unusual and meaningful.	☐ The organization is mostly clear, but some lapses occur. The ending is interesting.	☐ There is some organization, but it is unclear in places. The ending is not strong.	☐ There is little or no organization. The ending is not clear.
Conventions _____	☐ There are no errors in subject-verb agreement or verb tense.	☐ There are very few errors in subject-verb agreement or verb tense.	☐ There are errors in agreement and tense is not consistent.	☐ The writer fails to use conventions.

© Harcourt

Extended Writing/Test Prep

On the first two pages of this lesson, you will use what you have learned about sentence fluency and organization to write a longer written work.

A. **Read the three choices below. Put a star by the writing activity you would like to do.**

1. Respond to a Writing Prompt

Writing Situation: Your teacher is considering getting a pet for your classroom.

Directions for Writing: Think about what kind of an animal you would like to have in the classroom. Now, write a letter to convince your teacher that the animal you want is the best animal to get. You can also write to convince your teacher that an animal in the classroom is not a good idea. Remember to use different facts and reasons to support your opinion.

2. Choose one of the pieces of writing you started in this unit:

- a persuasive letter (page 130)

- a persuasive paragraph (page 136)

- a poem (page 142)

Revise and expand your draft into a complete piece of writing. Use what you have learned about sentence fluency and organization to write effectively.

3. Choose a topic you would like to write about. Write a narrative composition. Your narrative can be fiction or nonfiction.

B. **Use the space below and on the next page to plan your writing.**

TOPIC: _____

WRITING FORM: _____

HOW I WILL ORGANIZE MY WRITING: _____

_____

_____

_____

© Harcourt

Name _____

C. In the space below, draw a graphic organizer that will help you plan your writing. Fill in the graphic organizer. Write additional notes on the lines below.

Notes

_____

_____

_____

_____

_____

_____

_____

_____

D. Do your writing on another sheet of paper.

Name _____

Answering Multiple-Choice Questions

For questions on pages 154–157, fill in the bubble next to the correct answer.

A. Kyle made the plan below to organize ideas for a paper. Use his diagram to answer questions 1–3.

Kyle's Writing Plan

Opinion: Students should be allowed to bring cell phones to school.

Reason: Students need to communicate with family members before going home.

Fact: The pay phone closest to our school is four blocks away.

Fact: Using pay phones isn't very cool.

Fact: Four out of five students need to make transportation plans after school.

1. Which detail listed as a fact on Kyle's Writing Plan is actually an opinion?

   (A) Students take different kinds of transportation to school.

   (B) The pay phone closest to our school is four blocks away.

   (C) Using a pay phone isn't very cool.

   (D) Four out of five students need to make transportation plans after school.

2. Based on the information in Kyle's Writing Plan, what kind of paper is Kyle planning to write?

   (A) a paper that compares cell phones and pay phones

   (B) a letter that persuades school officials

   (C) a story about a student who doesn't have a cell phone

   (D) a poem about using a cell phone on a busy city street

3. Based on the information in Kyle's Writing Plan, which statement below is a reason that supports Kyle's main idea?

   (A) Using a pay phone is less expensive than using a cell phone.

   (B) Cell phones ring loudly and would disrupt class.

   (C) My cell phone is green and silver.

   (D) Studies show a positive link between cell phones and safety.

Test Tip:

A fact is a statistic or other statement that can be proven true. A reason is a statement that tells why the reader should agree with the writer. An opinion is a personal belief.

© Harcourt

B. The persuasive paragraph below is a first draft that Rachel wrote. The paragraph needs some revision. Read the paragraph to answer questions 1–3.

Let's Create a Community

(1) We need a community center in Bakersville now. (2) Bakersville is a great town, but it doesn't have a space to hold the kinds of organized activities the community needs. (3) At a community center, we could have sports leagues, family game nights, health fairs, an outdoor market, and movie screenings. (4) There are many highways in Bakersville that need to be repaired. (5) In a survey of the nearby city of Freedmont, 70% of the population said that the Freedmont Community Center was the most important service provided by the county. (6) So let's do three things. (7) Let's do them right away. (8) Think about a good location. (9) Discuss the idea at the next town hall meeting. (10) Won't you help me in this effort?

1. Which sentence is off topic and should be taken out of the paragraph?
   (A) sentence (2)
   (B) sentence (4)
   (C) sentence (7)
   (D) sentence (9)

> **Test Tip:**
> In an effective persuasive paragraph, a strong opinion statement is supported by facts, reasons, and personal experience. Ideas unrelated to the main idea should not be included.

2. Which two sentences would best be combined to make a compound sentence?
   (A) sentences (4) and sentence (5)
   (B) sentences (6) and sentence (7)
   (C) sentences (7) and sentence (8)
   (D) sentences (9) and sentence (10)

3. Which sentence should be added after sentence (8) to support the ideas in the paragraph?
   (A) Talk about how to raise money.
   (B) Visit Bakersville Community Center.
   (C) Buy balloons for the opening celebration.
   (D) Support Bakersville's high school football team.

© Harcourt

Name _____

C. **Read the poem. Choose the word or words that correctly complete
questions 1–3.**

Your Life

When you grow up you must decide

The role that's right for you.

You have to think before you ___(1)___

And to yourself be true.

If someone asks you to behave

Like a character you're not

Then tell them that the story ___(2)___ weak

And promptly change the plot.

Don't waste the chance to write your way

The most important tale of all.

You may not have chosen the setting of this play,

But the ___(3)___ is your call!

1. Which answer should go in blank (1)?

   (A) act

   (B) acts

   (C) acting

2. Which answer should go in blank (2)?

   (A) are

   (B) am

   (C) is

3. Which answer should go in blank (3)?

   (A) ending

   (B) ending's

   (C) endings

Test Tip:
Singular subjects
should have singular
verbs, and plural
subjects should
have plural verbs.
Use present tense
to tell about events
happening now, past
tense to tell about
events that have
already occurred, and
future tense to tell
about events that will
happen in the future.

Name _____

D. Read and answer questions 1–3.

1. Combine the sentences in the box to make one sentence.

> **Donnie visits his grandmother.**
>
> **Donnie takes his grandmother shopping.**

   Which sentence correctly combines the sentences in the box?
   - (A) After Donnie visits his grandmother goes shopping.
   - (B) Donnie visits his grandmother, and he takes her shopping.
   - (C) When Donnie goes shopping, and he takes his grandmother.

Test Tip:
You can vary sentence type and length by combining sentences. A sentence made up of two shorter sentences that are joined by a conjunction is a compound sentence.

2. Combine the sentences in the box to make one sentence.

> **Bryce washed the dishes after dinner.**
>
> **Bryce took out the trash after dinner.**
>
> **Bryce walked the dog after dinner.**

   Which sentence correctly combines the sentences in the box?
   - (A) After dinner, Bryce washed the dishes, took out the trash, and walked the dog.
   - (B) Bryce washed the dishes after dinner he took out the trash.
   - (C) After dinner washed the dishes, took out the trash, and walked the dog.

3. Combine the sentences in the box to make one sentence.

> **Jill and Dee sang a duet.**
>
> **Jill and Dee sang it at the concert.**

   Which sentence correctly combines the sentences in the box?
   - (A) Jill and Dee sang at the concert they sang a duet.
   - (B) Jill and Dee sang a duet at the concert.
   - (C) Jill or Dee sang a duet at the concert.

Name _____

Identify: More on Topics and Details

The **topic sentence** is the broadest, most general statement in a paragraph. It tells readers what the paragraph is about. Other sentences in the paragraph give **details** that tell more about the topic.

A. Read the following paragraph. Notice how the writer uses a general topic sentence. Also notice how he uses details to tell more about that topic.

Literature Model

Before they could cross the Rockies, the Corps of Discovery faced the Great Falls of the Missouri River in present-day Montana. Here the river tumbled down a bluff that was as high as a modern six-story building. The roar of the water was deafening. Lewis called it, "the grandest sight I ever beheld." But the waterfall meant that the explorers had to carry their boats and supplies up steep cliffs before they could set out again on quieter waters upstream. Traveling around the falls took the party twenty-four days, and left everyone exhausted.

—from *Lewis and Clark*
by R. Conrad Stein

B. Identify the topic sentence and details in the paragraph.
1. Underline the topic sentence of the paragraph.
2. Circle a detail sentence that tells Lewis's impression of the falls.
3. Put a box around another detail sentence that tells about the falls.

C. Explain why the Great Falls presented a challenge to the Corps of Discovery. Use information from the paragraph to support your ideas.

_____

_____

_____

_____

© Harcourt

Name _____

Explore: More on Topics and Details

Writers usually introduce the topic of a paragraph in the first sentence. The sentences that follow should contain facts, examples, and other details that make the topic clear for the readers.

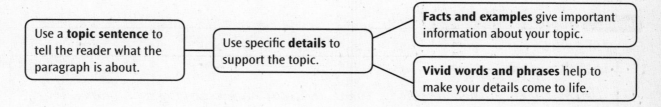

Use a **topic sentence** to tell the reader what the paragraph is about.

Use specific **details** to support the topic.

Facts and examples give important information about your topic.

Vivid words and phrases help to make your details come to life.

A. Read each topic sentence below. Then read each pair of detail sentences. Put a check next to the detail sentence that best supports the topic.

Example Topic: Veronica has a beautiful singing voice.

_____ She even listens to CDs when she studies.

✔ She can sing both high and low notes with a pretty tone.

1. Topic: Mount McKinley is the tallest mountain in North America.

_____ Mount McKinley stands 20,320 feet above sea level.

_____ Mountain climbers risk their lives to reach its top.

2. Topic: Many people think that all rats are mean and dirty creatures.

_____ You should buy your rat at a pet store with a good reputation.

_____ Rats often appear in the scary scenes of cartoons and movies.

3. Topic: Amanda's painting made me feel like I was in the Everglades.

_____ The saw grass looked like it was sprouting off the canvas.

_____ My parents and I visited the Everglades when I was eight years old.

B. Read the paragraph from *Lewis and Clark*. Underline the topic sentence. Then circle the two phrases that give supporting details.

In mid-September, a blinding snowstorm struck. Even the Shoshone guide got lost. Worst of all, the once-abundant wild game could not be found on the high mountain peaks.

C. Think about a place you would like to visit. Write a topic sentence and at least two details that tell about that place and why you would like to visit it. Use another sheet of paper.

Name _____

Use: More on Topics and Details

A **paragraph of explanation** tells what something is, how it works, or how it became what it is. Before you write a paragraph of explanation, think about your topic sentence and some supporting details. Here is how one student planned a paragraph that explains earthquakes.

Example Topic *earthquakes* _____

Ideas for Topic Sentence

When earthquakes happen, there is a lot more going on under the ground than you might realize.

Detail

Earth's crust has 14 pieces called plates.

Detail

Crust floats around on liquid mantle.

Detail

When plates rub against each other, they cause vibrations.

A. Think about something that happens in nature that you can explain. Write the topic on the line. Then complete the organizer.

Topic: _____

Ideas for Topic Sentence

Detail

Detail

Detail

B. Use information from your chart to draft a paragraph of explanation. Do your writing on another sheet of paper.

Name _____

The Parts of a Paragraph of Explanation

In a **paragraph of explanation** writers introduce a topic and use facts, examples, and other details to tell more about it. Here is an example of a paragraph of explanation written by a fifth grader. As you read, think about the writer's topic and the details that tell about it. Also think about how the student organized it. Then answer the questions.

Student Model

DRAFT

Earthquakes
by Terry

When earthquakes happen, there is a lot more going on under the ground than most people realize. The solid, top layer of Earth is called its crust. It is divided into fourteen huge plates, like a globe cut into fourteen jigsaw puzzle pieces. Right under the crust is a liquid layer called the mantle. The plates float around on the liquid mantle and sometimes rub up against each other. The vibrations make a low rumble. Then they shake the land near the edges of the plates that are being rubbed. Earthquakes only happen near fault lines. That is why there are more earthquakes in some parts of the world than others. An earthquake is simply the Earth readjusting itself.

Introduce the topic with a clear statement.

Develop the paragraph. Add details that support, illustrate, and explain the topic.

Organize your ideas and details. Arrange them in a logical order.

Be sure to use **irregular verbs** correctly.

Conclude by restating or summing up the main idea.

1. Which sentence introduces the topic? Underline it.
2. Which sentence gives a detail that tells the name of the Earth's top layer? Circle it.
3. Which sentence provides more information about that detail? Put a box around it.
4. Why are there more earthquakes in some parts of the world than others? Use details from the paragraph to explain why.

_____

_____

Name _____

Evaluate a Paragraph of Explanation

When you evaluate a paragraph of explanation, ask yourself how well the writer explained the topic. Also ask yourself how well the writer used details to support his or her ideas.

Now evaluate the Student Model. Put a check beside each thing the writer did well. If you do not think the writer did a good job, do not check the box.

- ☐ The writer introduced the topic with a clear statement.
- ☐ The writer organized the main details in a logical order.
- ☐ The writer developed the paragraph with details that support, illustrate, and explain the topic.
- ☐ The writer concluded the paragraph by restating or summing up the main idea.

Writer's Grammar
Irregular Verbs

Most verbs are regular. They form the past tense and past participle by adding –ed at the end of the verb (*I stop, I stopped, I have stopped*). **Irregular verbs** have special spellings for the past tense and past participle (*I see, I saw, I have seen*). The irregular verbs *be* and *have* also have special spellings for the present tense.

Example	Verb	Present	Past	Past Participle
	to be	am, are, is	were, was	(have, has, had) been
	to have	have, has	had	(have, has, had) had
	to see	see, sees	saw	(have, has, had) seen
	to do	do, does	did	(have, has, had) done
	to give	give, gives	gave	(have, has, had) given
	to teach	teach, teaches	taught	(have, has, had) taught

Complete each sentence with the correct past tense of the irregular verb in parentheses ( ).

1. We _____ a wonderful movie last night. (to see)

2. My father _____ math in high school and in college. (to teach)

3. He _____ extremely happy that he could help. (to be)

4. We _____ them a framed copy of the photograph. (to give)

© Harcourt

Name _____

Revise a Paragraph of Explanation: Adding Details

The writer could have improved his paragraph by adding descriptive details to support the topic. Here is how a detail sentence from the Student Model could have been improved.

Example **Read:** Earthquakes only happen near fault lines.

Ask Yourself: What are fault lines?

Improve the Sentence: _Earthquakes only happen near fault lines,_ _or near the edges of the plates._

A. Read this topic sentence from a paragraph of explanation a student wrote about checkers.

Checkers is a board game for two players.

Now read the following sentences. Rewrite them by adding details that support the main idea. Add other sentences as needed.

1. There are squares on the board.

   _____

2. The players set up their checkers.

   _____

   _____

3. The object of the game is to take your opponent's checkers.

   _____

   _____

B. Revise the draft of the paragraph of explanation you wrote on page 159. Be sure to improve your topic sentence and supporting sentences by adding more details. Also make sure to correctly spell any irregular verbs. Do you writing on another sheet of paper.

Name _____

Identify: Facts Versus Opinion

A **fact** is a statement that can be proven to be true. An **opinion** is a statement
that shows someone's feelings or thoughts.

A. Read the following passage. Notice how the writer included both facts and opinion.

Literature Model

Trudging behind her dogs, Kate traveled eight to ten grueling miles a day. When
she finally pulled into the tiny settlement of Glenora, eighty miles up the river, the news
spread fast: A white woman was in town! Not only that—she was as tall and strong as
the men who were packing supplies into the North, and she wore a broad-brimmed cow
driver's hat over her auburn curls. Jim Callbreath, a local resident who became Kate's
friend, said, "Any woman who could make it up to the Stikine River on the ice should be
treated as an equal to any packer in the territory."

—from *Klondike Kate*
by Liza Ketchum

B. Identify the facts and opinion in the passage.
   1. Underline a sentence that includes a fact about Kate's journey.
   2. Circle the phrase that gives a fact about the location of Glenora.
   3. Put a box around the opinion.

C. Using facts from the passage, explain why the people in Glenora found Kate unusual.

_____

_____

_____

_____

Name _____

Explore: Facts Versus Opinion

Writers use facts to give the reader information about a topic. Writers use opinions to share feelings, thoughts, or beliefs about the topic.

> A **fact** is a statement that can be proven to be true by checking a reliable source.

> An **opinion** cannot be proven. It is a statement that expresses feelings, thoughts, or beliefs.

> **Opinions** are not used in some writing forms, such as newspaper stories and essays that give historical information.

A. Read each pair of sentences below. Write "F" next to the one that expresses a fact. Write "O" next to the one that expresses an opinion.

Example   Rome is the capital of Italy, a country in southern Europe. _F_

Rome is the most beautiful city in the world. _O_

1. The first woman in space was Valentina Tereshkova, a Soviet cosmonaut. _____

   Valentina Tereshkova deserves respect for her hard work and dedication. _____

2. My grandfather's accomplishments should be an inspiration to all. _____

   My grandfather emigrated from Mexico when he was twenty years old. _____

3. John Coltrane was a jazz musician who played the saxophone. _____

   I believe that John Coltrane was the greatest saxophonist ever. _____

B. Read the passage from *Klondike Kate*. Underline one fact. Then circle the opinion.

> Her friends were appalled. Had she lost her mind? Women shouldn't travel alone to that part of the world—and how would she get there? Boats could only navigate the Yukon River in summer, and there were no roads or trains.

C. Write one fact about something that happened today. Then write a sentence that gives your opinion about the event.

Fact: _____

Opinion: _____

_____

Name _____

Use: Facts Versus Opinion

A **paragraph of historical information** tells about real events that happened
in the past. The writer usually arranges the events in time order. When you write
about historical information, try to separate facts from your personal opinions.
Here is how one student started to organize information for a paragraph about
a past event.

Example

Topic: *the first person to be hit by a meteorite*
Facts (can be proven to be true by checking an encyclopedia or textbook): *The meteorite hit her while she was taking a nap.* *The meteorite was the size of a grapefruit.*
Opinions (feelings or beliefs about the topic): *a miracle* *I hope it never happens to me.*

A. Think about a historical event that interests you. It can be an event that you have read
about or one that you have heard about from a reliable source. Then fill out the chart.

Topic:
Facts (can be proven to be true by checking an encyclopedia or textbook):
Opinions (feelings or beliefs about the topic):

B. Now use only the facts from the chart to write a draft about a historical event. Describe the
event in time order. Do your writing on another sheet of paper.

Name _____

The Parts of a Paragraph of Historical Information

A **paragraph of historical information** tells about a real event. The paragraph is developed with details that usually are arranged in time order. Here is an example of a paragraph of historical information written by a fifth grader. As you read, think about how the student organized it. Then answer the questions.

Student Model

DRAFT

**The Meteorite and Mrs. Hodges
by Tamara**

Mrs. Ann Hodges, who lived in Alabama, was the first and only known person to be hit by a meteorite and to live to tell the tale. The day was November 30, 1954. A meteorite the size of a grapefruit crashed through the roof of Mrs. Hodge's home. People as far as Georgia and Mississippi reported seeing a flash of light as the meteorite streaked through the atmosphere. It crashed through the living room ceiling, where Mrs. Hodges was taking a nap on the couch. Then the meteorite smashed into a radio and toward Mrs. Hodges, where it struck her in the hip. She was able to walk afterwards, which I think is a miracle. She suffered severe bruises, but she was able to enjoy a little bit of celebrity.

> Introduce the historical event with a **topic sentence.**

> Arrange the events in **time order.**

> **Develop** the paragraph. Add details that support, illustrate, and explain the topic.

> Include only **facts,** not opinions.

> Avoid using **contractions.**

> **Conclude** by summing up the topic of the paragraph.

1. Which sentence introduces the topic of the paragraph? Underline it.
2. Which sentence develops the paragraph by stating a fact about how the meteorite hit Mrs. Hodges? Put a box around it.
3. Find the writer's opinion about the event. Underline it twice. Explain how you know it is an opinion.

_____

_____

_____

© Harcourt

Name _____

Evaluate a Paragraph of Historical Information

When you evaluate a paragraph of historical information, ask yourself how well the writer used facts to develop the topic. Also ask yourself if the writer avoided using personal opinions about the topic.

Now evaluate the Student Model. Put a check beside each thing the writer did well. If you do not think the writer did a good job, do not check the box.

- ☐ The writer introduced the historical event with a topic sentence.
- ☐ The writer arranged the events in time order.
- ☐ The writer used details to support, illustrate, and explain the topic.
- ☐ The writer used only facts and did not include opinions.
- ☐ The writer concluded by summing up the topic of the paragraph.

Writer's Grammar

Contractions

A **contraction** is the shortened form of two or more words. An apostrophe (')
is used to replace the letter or letters that are taken out. The word *not* is often
combined with a verb in a contraction. Contractions should not be used in
formal writing.

you've = you + have	**you'll** = you + will
doesn't = does + not	**haven't** = have + not

Correct each sentence. Change the contraction in parentheses to the correct long form.

1. (It's) _____ difficult to appreciate some art.

2. The Empire State Building (isn't) _____ the tallest building in the United States.

3. I (can't) _____ believe that the Watts Towers were almost torn down.

4. Washington, D.C. (hasn't) _____ always been the capital of the United States.

5. (You're) _____ about to learn about the greatest athlete in the world.

Name _____

Revise a Paragraph of Historical Information: Deleting Opinions

One way the writer could have improved the paragraph of historical information was by leaving out opinions. Here is how a sentence from the Student Model could be improved by deleting the opinion.

Example **Read:** "She was able to walk afterwards, which I think is a miracle."

Ask Yourself: How does the writer express an opinion in this sentence?

Think: The writer describes how she feels about the event. To avoid using her opinion, the writer should have only included the factual details.

Improve the Sentence: _She was able to walk afterwards._

A. Revise the following sentences by deleting the opinions and using only the facts.

1. I was surprised that Jessica Miller finished in first place and set a new school record.

   _____

2. I think it was a bad idea for the explorers to build a fort in the middle of a mosquito-infested swamp.

   _____

3. It is sad that the architect did not get to see the completed house she had designed for her husband.

   _____

4. Last night the drama club performed *The Loon's Last Call,* which I thought was hilarious.

   _____

B. Revise the draft of a paragraph of historical information that you wrote on page 166. Be sure to delete any opinions and change any contractions to the correct long form. Do your writing on another sheet of paper.

© Harcourt

Name _____

Identify: Putting Ideas in Sequence

Putting ideas in sequence means organizing ideas in the order in which they happen. Good writers use transition words, such as *first, then, next,* and *finally,* to make the sequence of events clear.

A. Read the following passage. Notice how the writer puts his ideas in sequence.

Literature Model

It can take more than twelve hours to climb to the top from Camp 4. Since it's critical to make it back to camp before dark, climbers usually set out before midnight, and climb through the night by the light of a headlamp. With luck, these climbers will be on top the following noon.

—from *The Top of the World: Climbing Mount Everest*
by Steve Jenkins

B. Identify the sequence of ideas in the passage.

1. Underline the part of a sentence that describes the first stage of the climb to the top from Camp 4.

2. Circle the part of a sentence that describes the second stage of the climb.

3. Put a box around the sentence that describes the third stage of the climb.

C. In your own words, describe the sequence of steps that the climbers must take to climb to the top of the mountain from Camp 4. Use transition words, such as *first, then, next,* and *finally,* to make the sequence of events clear.

_____

_____

_____

Name _____

Explore: Putting Ideas in Sequence

Writers put ideas in sequence to describe a series of events or to explain how to do something. Transition words help writers show time-order sequence.

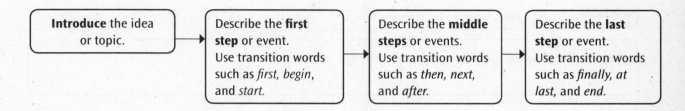

Introduce the idea or topic.	Describe the **first step** or event. Use transition words such as *first, begin,* and *start*.	Describe the **middle steps** or events. Use transition words such as *then, next,* and *after*.	Describe the **last step** or event. Use transition words such as *finally, at last,* and *end*.

A. Read the paragraph. Then circle the transition words that let readers know the sequence of ideas. The first one is circled for you.

My father showed me how to cook a pot of rice for dinner. (First,) he measured 3 cups of water and poured it into a pot on the stove. Second, he turned on the stove to boil the water. After the water reached a boil, he added $1\frac{1}{2}$ cups of rice and covered the pot with a lid. Then he let the rice simmer for 15 minutes. Finally, he turned the burner off and waited another 15 minutes before scooping it onto our plates.

B. Explain how to prepare your favorite snack. Use transition words and phrases to put your ideas in a clear sequence.

_____

_____

_____

_____

_____

_____

Name _____

Use: Putting Ideas in Sequence

A **how-to paragraph** explains how to make or do something. The steps to follow are arranged in time order. Here is how one student planned to explain how to plant tomatoes.

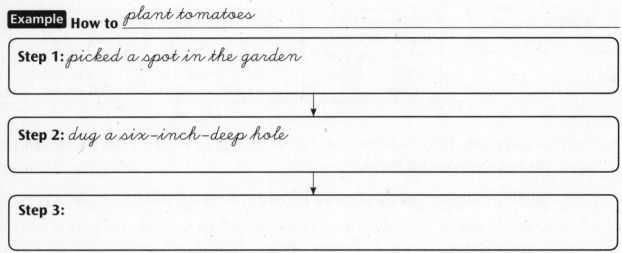

Example How to _plant tomatoes_

Step 1: _picked a spot in the garden_

Step 2: _dug a six-inch-deep hole_

Step 3:

A. Think about something that you recently learned to do or make. Use the organizer below to put your ideas in sequence.

How to _____

Step 1:

Step 2:

Step 3:

B. Use the information from your chart to draft a how-to paragraph. Use transition words or phrases to help show the time order. Do your writing on another sheet of paper.

Name _____

The Parts of a How-to Paragraph

In a **how-to paragraph,** the writer gives step-by-step directions for how to do or make something. Here is an example of a how-to paragraph written by a fifth-grade student. As you read, think about how the student organized the steps that were followed. Then answer the questions.

Student Model

Planting Tomatoes
by Jonas

    My grandmother taught me two things last summer—that I like tomatoes and that I like planting them even more! First, we picked a spot in her garden where the tomato plants would get plenty of sunlight. Then we dug a six-inch-deep hole for each plant and put a handful of compost in each. The compost acts as a fertilizer, so the plants will have enough nutrients to grow big, juicy tomatoes. Next, we careful poured some water in each hole. Then we put a young tomato plant in each one. We covered the roots with dirt and watered them one last time. Finally, after we had put all the plants in the soil, it was time to wait and watch them grow. We eventually picked the grown tomatoes, and they tasted great because we grew them ourselves.

Introduce the topic. Begin with an exciting first sentence to catch readers' interest.

Organize your paragraph. Discuss each step in time-order sequence.

Develop your paragraph. Include transitions that put the ideas in sequence.

Use **adverbs,** such as *finally,* to describe when actions take place.

Conclude by reminding your readers what they have learned.

1. Which sentence introduces the topic? Underline it.
2. What does the writer wish to explain with the paragraph?

_____

_____

3. Which transition words or phrases does the writer use to organize the sequence of steps? Circle them.
4. Which sentence concludes the paragraph? Put a box around it.

© Harcourt

Name _____

Evaluate a How-to Paragraph

A how-to paragraph gives clear step-by-step directions for how to do or make something. When you evaluate a how-to paragraph, ask yourself how well the writer put the ideas in sequence. Also ask yourself whether the writer used transition words to clarify the sequence of steps or events.

Now evaluate the Student Model. Put a check beside each thing the writer did well. If you do not think the writer did a good job, do not check the box.

- ☐ The writer introduced the topic with a first sentence that caught readers' interest.
- ☐ The writer organized the paragraph in time-order sequence.
- ☐ The writer used transition words to help show the sequence of ideas.
- ☐ The writer concluded by reminding readers what they learned.

Writer's Grammar

Adverbs

An **adverb** is a word that tells about a verb, an adjective, or another adverb. Adverbs often tell *how* (happily), *when* (last), or *where* (inside). Transition words that describe *when* sometimes are adverbs.

Complete the paragraph with the correct adverb from the Word Bank.

Example Why buy a piñata when you can ___*easily*___ make one at home?

To get started, you need water, flour, a bowl, newspaper, and a big balloon. _____, mix $\frac{1}{2}$ cup of flour and 2 cups of warm water in the bowl. _____ tear the newspaper _____ into long strips and dip them in the water. Wrap the wet strips around the balloon, covering it _____. When you are done adding layers, place the balloon in a _____ warm place. After the paper dries, pop the balloon and fill the space with candy. _____, you are ready to decorate your new piñata.

Word Bank

completely
easily
finally
first
length-wise
somewhat
then

© Harcourt

Name _____

Revise a How-to Paragraph: Proofreading

The writer could have improved his paragraph by proofreading it for errors. Here is an example of how a sentence from the Student Model could have been improved.

Example Next, we careful‸poured some water in each hole.
                                    ly

Next, we carefully poured some water in each hole.

A. Revise these sentences by proofreading. Use proofreading marks to mark the error in each sentence. Then rewrite the sentence on the lines.

1. Be extreme careful when you open the present.

   _____

2. After the stop sign, turn right on Melvin street.

   _____

3. You should know immediately if you have done your job good.

   _____

4. I wouldnt worry if the muffins aren't perfect the first time.

   _____

5. You might have been afraid the first time you rided a horse.

   _____

B. Revise the draft of a how-to paragraph that you wrote on page 172. Be sure to proofread for errors in spelling, capitalization, and punctuation. Also make sure check that you used adverbs correctly. Do your writing on another sheet of paper.

> **Word Bank**
> **Proofreading Marks**
> ℰ delete text
> ^ insert text
> [move text
> = capitalize
> / lowercase

Writer's Companion • UNIT 6
Lesson 28 Putting Ideas in Sequence

Name _____

Review Writer's Craft

You have learned how to introduce a topic with a topic sentence and to use details to support the main idea. You have also learned to recognize the difference between facts and opinions and how to organize your writing by putting ideas in sequence.

A. Read the following passage. Notice how the writer uses a topic sentence and details, facts and opinion, and sequence.

Literature Model

Neil and Buzz stay on the moon for 21 hours and 36 minutes, but only a little more than 2 hours of that time is spent outside the lunar module. They perform three minor experiments and load two aluminum suitcases with 48 pounds (22 kilograms) of moon dust and rocks.

When they have climbed back into the lunar module and shut the hatch, they take their helmets off. They look at each other because they both sense a strong smell. Neil thinks it smells like wet ashes. Buzz says it smells like spent gunpowder. It is the moon. The moon has a smell.

—from *The Man Who Went to the Far Side of the Moon*
by Bea Uusma Schyffert

B. Identify topic sentences, details, facts, and opinions.
1. Underline the sentence in the first paragraph that introduces the topic.
2. Circle the detail that supports the topic sentence of the first paragraph.
3. Put a box around Neil's and Buzz's opinions about how the moon smells.

C. Using transition words, summarize the sequence of events in the second paragraph.

_____

_____

_____

_____

Name _____

Review Writer's Craft

You can use ideas and conventions to explain how something happened or exactly how you feel about a topic.

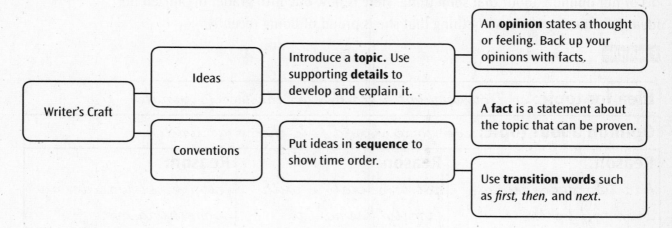

A. Read the following passage from *The Man Who Went to the Far Side of the Moon*. Notice how the writer organizes her ideas.

> Down on the ground, one million people are squinting at the spacecraft, now just a spot in the sky, watching it get smaller and smaller. Within moments it is lost from sight. Then it is gone altogether. People get up, fold their blankets, and head for their cars, going home or back to work. Everything is back to normal again. For everyone, except for three people.

B. Use the paragraph above to complete the activity.
1. Underline the topic sentence.
2. Circle two details that support the topic sentence.
3. Put a box around the transition words or phrases that the writer uses to help show the sequence of events.

C. Write one fact and one opinion that could be added to the passage.

Fact: _____

_____

Opinion: _____

_____

Name _____

Review Writer's Craft

In an **essay of explanation,** the writer explains what something is, how something happens, or how something is done. The writer also can use details to give reasons for his or her opinion about that something. Here is how one fifth grader organized her ideas for an essay about something that she is proud of doing recently.

Example

Idea for topic: *collecting winter clothes for the less fortunate*		
Opinion about topic: *everyone should help the community*		
Reason: *had fun decorating drop-off boxes*	**Reason:** *got to socialize with family friends at dinner*	**Reason:** *felt like I was doing something nice*
Details: *used creativity to decorate them*	**Details:** *asked permission to place boxes in front of family friends' businesses*	**Details:** *collected the donations and gave them to an organization*

A. Answer the following questions about the chart.

   1. Using the information in the chart, write a topic sentence that the writer could use in this essay.

   _____

   _____

   2. Write a sentence that gives one reason why the writer thinks everyone should help the community. Use information from the chart to back up that opinion.

   _____

   _____

B. Use the details in the chart to write two sentences about collecting winter clothes. Use transition words or phrases to put the ideas in sequence. Do your writing on another sheet of paper.

Name _____

The Parts of an Essay of Explanation

In an **essay of explanation,** a writer introduces a topic and organizes details about it. Here is a draft of an essay of explanation written by a fifth grader. As you read, think about how the student organized it. Then answer the questions.

Student Model

Making the Winter Warmer
by Tanya

This fall I collected winter clothes for less fortunate people in our community. The whole process was a great way to help people in need.

First, some friends and I had fun decorating the drop-off boxes. We used our creativity by making the big cardboard boxes stand out. We painted each box with eye-catching colors and drew signs that invited people to donate coats and jackets they no longer wore.

The next morning, my father and I placed the boxes in front of the businesses of our family friends. Before we did, we asked the friends over to our house for a special "request" dinner. Then my father and I returned twice a week to collect the donations. Finally, we gave the clothes to an organization that distributed them to the people who needed them most.

It felt good to collect those donations. I couldn't exactly make the winter warmer, but I knew I made some people warmer. I think that everyone should help the community, because one person can really make a difference.

> **Introduce** the topic with an interesting first paragraph.

> **Organize** by arranging the main points logically. Put the ideas in sequence and use transition words such as *first* and *next*.

> **Develop** your topic. Provide reasons for your opinions. Back up your reasons with facts and details.

> **Conclude** by restating or summing up the topic in the last paragraph.

1. Which paragraph introduces the topic of the essay? Underline it.
2. Why did the writer have a great time decorating the drop-off boxes? Circle the reason.
3. What transition words and phrases does the writer use to organize the sequence of events? Put boxes around them.
4. What step is not in time order? Underline it twice. Then draw an arrow to show where it belongs in correct time order.

© Harcourt

Evaluate an Essay of Explanation

A. Students were asked to write an essay of explanation about why they are proud of something they did recently. The letter below received a score of 4. When using a 4-point rubric, a score of 4 means "excellent." Read the essay of explanation and the comments to find out why this essay is a success.

Student Model

Saturdays with the Elderly
by Samuel

To be honest, it was my mother's idea. She nearly had to drag me there. Now, after only two weeks, I am dragging her. I never would have guessed that volunteering my Saturday mornings at a home for the elderly could be so much fun.

> Nice introduction! The first paragraph really makes the reader want to read more.

My morning begins in the cafeteria where I eat breakfast with the residents. Before I am even sitting, they start telling the most amazing stories. Mr. Anderson, for example, told me stories from a summer he spent riding his bicycle from Atlanta, Georgia, to Los Angeles, California—with his pet cat, Lucky! Before I knew it, an hour had passed.

> Good work. You organize your essay in time order, using transitions to show the sequence of events.

After breakfast we all move to the activity room. There some people play a confusing card game called bridge, while the others play checkers or read magazines. I like to play checkers, usually with Mrs. Green, who beats me every time. It may sound strange, but it is fun to lose to Mrs. Green. Right when I think I am about to win, she will suddenly take half of my checkers and then stand up and do a funny victory dance.

> Nice job! You use interesting details to support the main idea and the topic of each paragraph.

My time volunteering at the home for the elderly has taught me to be open to new experiences, even if they might not sound exciting at first. If I am proud of anything, it is that I am able to have fun doing something that other kids might think is boring.

> Nice conclusion. You sum up your essay thoughtfully.

© Harcourt

Name _____

Evaluating the Student Model

B. This essay received a score of 2. Why did it get a low score?

Student Model

The End, at Last
by Alexandra

I can play the piano.

At first, I had difficulty reading and playing the notes at the same time. I became familiar with the piece of music, and it actually sounded like my left hand and my right hand were playing from the same sheet of music!

When I am practicing, I sometimes get distracted and lose my concentration. To me it is easier to start at the beginning than to start from the middle. As a result, it was very difficult for me to reach the end of the piece.

It took a long time, but all the practice paid off.

> You should include a whole paragraph that introduces your topic.

> You organized this paragraph by putting the events in time order but need more transition words to make the sequence of events more clear.

> These details do not support your topic very well. Find others to use.

> You conclude your essay, but you should use more details to sum up the topic.

C. What score would you give the essay? Put a number on each line.

	4	3	2	1
Ideas _____	☐ The writing is completely focused on a topic that is supported by strong, specific details.	☐ The writing is somewhat focused on a topic that is supported by details.	☐ The writing is related to the topic and has few supporting details.	☐ The writing is not related to the topic and has no supporting details.
Conventions _____	☐ The ideas are in a logical sequence. Transition words make the relationships clear.	☐ The sequence is mostly clear. Some transition words are used.	☐ The sequence is unclear in some places. Few or no transition words are used.	☐ There is little or no sequence. No transition words are used.
Conventions _____	☐ All irregular verbs, contractions, and adverbs are used correctly.	☐ There are few errors in the use of irregular verbs, contractions, or adverbs.	☐ There are some errors in the use of irregular verbs, contractions, or adverbs.	☐ There are many errors in the use of irregular verbs, contractions, and adverbs.

Extended Writing/Test Prep

On the first two pages of this lesson, you will use what you have learned about topic sentences and details, fact and opinion, and sequence of ideas to write a longer work.

A. **Read the three choices below. Put a star by the writing activity you would like to do.**

1. Respond to a Writing Prompt

   Writing Situation: Everyone has succeeded at something.

   Directions for Writing: Think about something that you have done successfully. Now write an essay of explanation that explains how you succeeded. Tell your story in sequence and use details and examples.

2. Choose one of the pieces of writing you started in this unit:

   • a paragraph of explanation (page 160)

   • a paragraph of historical information (page 166)

   • a how-to paragraph (page 172)

   Revise and expand your draft into a complete piece of writing. Use what you have learned about ideas and conventions.

3. Choose a topic you would like to write about. You may write a paragraph or essay of explanation, a paragraph of historical information, or a how-to paragraph. Be sure to support your topic with details. Use facts and opinions when they are appropriate. Also remember to put your ideas in sequence.

B. **Use the space below and on the next page to plan your writing.**

TOPIC: _____

WRITING FORM: _____

HOW WILL I ORGANIZE MY WRITING: _____

_____

_____

_____

© Harcourt

Name _____

C. In the space below, draw a graphic organizer that will help you plan your writing. Fill in the graphic organizer. Write additional notes on the lines below.

Notes

_____

_____

_____

_____

_____

_____

D. Do your writing on another sheet of paper.

Answering Multiple-Choice Questions

For questions on pages 184–187, fill in the bubble next to the correct answer.

A. Monica made the plan below to organize ideas for a paper. Use her plan to answer questions 1–3.

Monica's Writing Plan

How to Make a collage

Step 1: *Find pictures in old magazines.*

Step 2: *Read the interesting articles.*

Step 3: *Use scissors to cut out pictures.*

Step 4: *Apply glue to backs of the pictures.*

1. Based on the information in Monica's Writing Plan, which detail below could be added as a Step 5 for the sequence of ideas?
   - (A) Ask your parents for old magazines.
   - (B) Hang the collage on your wall.
   - (C) Put the pictures on a sheet of poster board.
   - (D) Show your finished product to your friends.

Test Tip:
The steps should appear in time order.

2. Which step from Monica's Writing Plan is off topic and should be removed from the plan?
   - (A) Find pictures in old magazines.
   - (B) Read the interesting articles.
   - (C) Use scissors to cut out pictures.
   - (D) Apply glue to backs of the pictures.

3. Based on the information in Monica's Writing Plan, what kind of paper is Monica planning to write?
   - (A) a paper that provides historical information on collages
   - (B) a paper that explains why she likes collages
   - (C) a paper that tells a story about making a collage
   - (D) a paper that explains how to make a collage

© Harcourt

Name _____

B. The paragraph below is a first draft that Billy wrote. The paragraph
contains mistakes. Read the story to answer questions 1–3.

Shoveling Snow

(1) It hardly ever snows in Jacksonville, Florida. (2) This winter I shoveled
snow for the first time when I was visiting my grandparents in Brooklyn,
New York. (3) At first, I volunteered to shovel the snow off their steps, which
was easy and fun. (4) After my grandfather saw how good of a job I did, he
asked me to shovel the snow off the sidewalk. (5) Shoveling the snow off the
neighbor's steps wasn't nearly as easy or fun because I was so exhausted.
(6) Then, a neighbor saw me shoveling the snow off the sidewalk and offered
to pay me to shovel the snow off her steps! (7) I could not refuse. (8) I hope I
never have to shovel snow again!

1. Which sentence expresses the writer's opinion?
   - (A) sentence (1)
   - (B) sentence (2)
   - (C) sentence (3)
   - (D) sentence (6)

> **Test Tip:**
> An opinion is what
> the writer feels or
> thinks about a topic.

2. Sentence (5) does not follow the sequence of events. Where should
   it be placed to keep the events in order?
   - (A) before sentence (2)
   - (B) before sentence (3)
   - (C) before sentence (7)
   - (D) before sentence (8)

3. Which sentence below could be added after sentence (1) to give
   details that support the topic and sequence of the paragraph?
   - (A) Jacksonville is a city in northeast Florida.
   - (B) I always thought that it would be fun to shovel snow.
   - (C) The neighbor also asked me to shovel the sidewalk in front of her house.
   - (D) Now I hope it never snows in Jacksonville!

Name _____

C. Read the paragraph, "Rats!" Choose the word or words that correctly completes questions 1–4.

Rats!

Many people are terrified by rats and could never imagine keeping one as a pet. What these people _____(1)_____ know is that rats are rodents and that some rodents can make wonderful pets. Guinea pigs are the best example, and there are many reasons why they make great pets. First of all, they are quite intelligent creatures. Guinea pigs _____(2)_____ so smart that, like cats, you can train them to use a litter box. Secondly, guinea pigs are very social and love to play with humans. Like a dog or a cat, a guinea pig will even _____(3)_____ lick its owner's hand when it is petted. Finally, guinea pigs don't need a lot of space. You can keep them comfortable in a medium-sized cage. If all these reasons sound good, then maybe _____(4)_____ ready to let a rodent—or at least a guinea pig—into your home!

1. Which answer should go in blank (1)?

Ⓐ doesn't

Ⓑ don't

Ⓒ do'nt

2. Which answer should go in blank (2)?

Ⓐ are

Ⓑ be

Ⓒ is

3. Which answer should go in blank (3)?

Ⓐ affection

Ⓑ affectionate

Ⓒ affectionately

4. Which answer should go in blank (4)?

Ⓐ your

Ⓑ your'e

Ⓒ you're

> **Test Tip:**
>
> A contraction is two words combined into one with an apostrophe (').
>
> The apostrophe fills in the place where there are missing letters.
>
> **have + not = haven't**

© Harcourt

Name _____

D. Read and answer questions 1–4.

1. Read the sentence below.

> Aunt Jessie <u>brung</u> over some food for dinner.

Which type of mistake appears in the underlined section of the sentence?

- (A) Punctuation error
- (B) Capitalization error
- (C) Usage error

2. Read the sentence below.

> Did the sailboat sail the length <u>of the Mississippi river?</u>

Which type of mistake appears in the underlined section of the sentence?

- (A) Punctuation error
- (B) Capitalization error
- (C) Spelling error

3. Read the sentence below.

> "<u>Thier seats</u> are in the very front row."

Which type of mistake appears in the underlined section of the sentence?

- (A) Spelling error
- (B) Capitalization error
- (C) Punctuation error

4. Read the sentence below.

> This weekend, <u>I played good</u> at the soccer tournament.

Which type of mistake appears in the underlined section of the sentence?

- (A) Spelling error
- (B) Usage error
- (C) Capitalization error

Test Tip:

The words *good* and *bad* are adjectives. Adjectives modify, or describe, a noun or pronoun.

The word well is an adverb. Adverbs modify, or describe, verbs, adjectives, or other adverbs.

© Harcourt

Parts of Speech

The parts of speech are the different kinds of words you use in sentences.

Nouns are words that name people, places, and things. They can name things that can be seen or touched. They also can name things that cannot be seen or touched.

Proper nouns are nouns that name a special person, place, or thing.

> **Mr. Henderson** (person) wants to sail down the **Mississippi River** (place) in the world-famous **Old Time Steamboat** (thing).

Common nouns name any person, place, or thing.

> I just saw my **aunt** (person) walking to **town** (place) and holding her favorite **umbrella** (thing) in case it rains.

Compound nouns are made up of more than one word. Compound nouns may be separated by hyphens, combined to make a new word, or separated by a space.

> When I was young, I always got my sisters' **hand-me-downs** instead of new clothes. But I didn't care. I knew when I was an adult, I'd just go **outside,** drive my **station wagon** to the store, and pick out new clothes that I bought with my own money.

Verbs are words that show an action or tell what something is or is like.

> Matt and Lauren **flew** to San Francisco. (action)
> Liz **was** delighted to see them. (tells what the subject is)

Verbs have **tenses**. Tenses show *when* an action takes place—the present, the past, or the future.

> I **sing** in the school chorus. (present tense)
> I **sang** in the school chorus last year. (past tense)
> I **will sing** in the school chorus next year. (future tense)

Action verbs tell what someone is doing, has done, or will do.

> Jack **grew** a wonderful beanstalk.
> It **will get** even taller.

Linking verbs tell how someone or something feels or thinks or what a person, place, or thing is like. Linking verbs are often forms of *to be*, such as *am*, *is*, and *are*.

> Jack **is** very happy about his giant beanstalk.
> Jack **seemed** surprised by the height of the beanstalk.
> It **looked** huge in front of his small house.

© Harcourt

Pronouns are words that take the place of nouns. There are several types of pronouns.

Subject pronouns are pronouns that act as the subject of a sentence. (See **Subjects**.)

The Barrymore family moved last week. **They** put all of their furniture inside a huge truck.

Object pronouns are pronouns that receive the action of a verb.

Where is that suitcase? I can't remember where I put **it**.

Possessive pronouns are pronouns that show ownership.

The bat found **its** new home in the attic.

Adjectives are words that describe, or **modify**, a noun or a pronoun.

You are a **funny** person because you tell **clever** jokes.

Articles are a special type of adjective. *A*, *an*, and *the* are articles. Articles come before nouns, and they answer the question *Which one?*

An island in **a** lake is **the** place where I would like to be.

Adverbs also are words that describe, or **modify**. Most adverbs describe verbs. Sometimes adverbs describe adjectives or other adverbs.

The students **quickly** headed to the cafeteria. They were **very** hungry for lunch.

Prepositions are words that link a noun or pronoun to another word in the sentence.

Will you have lunch **with** me this afternoon?
We will eat **at** the table **in** the corner **of** the lunchroom.

Conjunctions are words that join words or groups of words. **And**, **but**, and **or** are conjunctions.

We could eat at noon, **or** we could eat at one o'clock.
Jana **or** Maria will join us.

Sentences

A sentence is a group of words that tells a complete thought.

Complete sentences have both a subject and a predicate. They express a complete thought.

Kara and I went to visit the Statue of Liberty last week.

Subjects name whom or what a sentence is about. The subject of a sentence usually is a noun or a pronoun.

Barney joined in the applause.
He enjoys going to concerts.

A **compound subject** names two or more people, places, or things.

Ina and Maria are sisters.

Predicates tell what action the subject of a sentence does. The predicate has a verb in it.

The audience **gave the band an ovation**.

A **compound predicate** has two or more verbs.

The sisters **dance and sing**.

Simple sentences are made up of a single independent clause. Simple sentences can be short or long. They can have compound subjects or compound predicates. Below, the subjects are underlined once. The verbs are underlined twice.

One subject and verb: The sun rose.
Compound subject: The sun and clouds were in the sky.
Compound verb: The moon rose and shone last night.
Compound subject and compound verb: The boy and girl thought it over and decided to bring raincoats.

Compound sentences are made up of two or more independent clauses. The independent clauses are usually joined by a comma and a conjunction such as *and*, *but*, *for*, *nor*, *or so*, or *yet*.

Flags were displayed all over the arena, **but** the Olympic athletes had not yet appeared.

Fragments are incomplete sentences. You correct them and make them complete by adding a subject or a predicate.

FRAGMENT: Finding a place to sit.
COMPLETE: Finding a place to sit **is part of the game of "Musical Chairs."**

FRAGMENT: Bought a red car.
COMPLETE: **The Jackson family** bought a red car.

© Harcourt

Combining sentences makes a single sentence out of two or more sentences. It makes writing flow and keeps it interesting. Use a conjunction to join the subject and predicate parts of the sentence or to join parts of the subject or predicate.

> Two short sentences: I like riding on roller coasters. I enjoy Ferris wheels.
> Combined sentence: I like riding on roller coasters, and I enjoy Ferris wheels.

> Two short sentences: Robin enjoys jogging. Fern enjoys jogging.
> Combined sentence: Robin and Fern enjoy jogging.

Run-On Sentences A run-on sentence puts two ideas together incorrectly. Run-on sentences sometimes have a comma in them, and sometimes they have no punctuation. The two ideas should be either joined or separated by correct punctuation.

> RUN-ON: The girls ran into the gym, they had to do fifty sit-ups on the mats.
> CORRECTED: The girls ran into the gym. They had to do fifty sit-ups on the mats. (separated by an end mark, such as a period, question mark, or exclamation point)

> RUN-ON: I prefer to climb the rope I'm always the first one in line.
> CORRECTED: I prefer to climb the rope, **and** I'm always the first one in line. (joined with a comma and a conjunction)

Capitalization and Punctuation

Capitalization is used to emphasize the important words in a sentence. It helps make sentences easier for the reader to understand.

First Word in a Sentence The first word in a sentence is always capitalized.

> **Can** you help me find my house key?

Proper nouns, as well as the pronoun *I*, are always capitalized.

> My aunt **Harriet** in **Detroit** and **I** talked on the phone last night.

Punctuation refers to symbols, or marks, that help a reader know how to read a sentence.

End Marks are used at the end of a complete sentence.

Periods are used to end declarative sentences, which make a statement. They also are used to end imperative sentences that make a polite request.

> There is a meeting of the track club after school today.
> Please come, if you are interested in the club.

Question marks are used to end interrogative sentences, which ask a question.

> Will you come to the meeting**?**

Exclamation points are used to end sentences and short statements that show strong emotion.

> Give that back!
> No! Stop that!

Commas are used to show a brief pause. Here are a few rules to remember about commas.

Commas are used with **compound sentences**.

> Jana and Dot wrote stories, and then they decided to publish them.

Commas are used to separate **items in a series** of three or more items.

> The colors of the American flag are red, white, and blue.

Commas are used to **separate adjectives that are equal in their importance**. You can test this rule by changing the order of the adjectives. If the meaning of the sentence is unchanged, the adjectives are equal in importance.

> Yuri chose a long, blue jacket to wear to the dance.
> (You can also write *Yuri chose a blue, long jacket to wear to the dance* without changing the meaning of the sentence.)

© Harcourt

Commas are *not* used to separate adjectives that must stay in a specific order.

> Jane wore a bright yellow shirt.
> (You cannot write *Jane wore a yellow bright shirt*.)

Commas are used sometimes **to introduce ideas in a sentence**.

> First, we will need to beat two eggs.

Colons are used to in very several situations.

> To introduce a list–The following visitors attended the modern art exhibit today: school children, foreign travelers, and senior citizens.
> To give the time–It is 4:08 P.M.
> To begin a business letter–To Whom it May Concern:

Quotation Marks are used to show when people are speaking. Periods and commas are always placed inside final quotation marks.

> Tamara said, "I have had enough hiking for today."
> "We had a good time, though," she admitted.

Italics give special emphasis to words. They are also used for certain kinds of titles, such as the titles of books.

> The word *illuminate* comes from a Latin root that means "to light."
> *Oliver Twist* is just one of Charles Dickens's books that has been made into a film.

Apostrophes are used to show ownership. Apostrophes are also used in contractions.

Add an apostrophe and an *s* to show the possessive of most singular nouns, even when the noun ends in an *s*.

> The mitt of the baseball player = The baseball player**'s** mitt
> The view from the lens = The len**s's** view

Add only an apostrophe to show the possessive of plural nouns that end in -*s* or -*es*.

> The color of the blueberries = The blueberries**'** color

Add an apostrophe and an *s* to show the possessive of plural nouns that do not end in *s* or *es*.

> The project of the children = The children**'s** project

Apostrophes can take the place of a missing letter or letters. (See **Contractions**)

> are not = aren**'**t
> I am = I**'**m
> he would = he**'**d

Abbreviations are shortened versions of words or phrases. They are used for titles, the names of states, and measurements. Most, but not all, abbreviations end in periods.

Mister = **Mr.**
New Jersey = **NJ** (no period)
Avenue = **Ave.**
teaspoons = **tsp.**
millimeters = **mm** (no period)

Usage

Usage refers to how words and sentences are used in speaking or writing.

Plural Nouns The plural form refers to more than one person, place or thing. There are two kinds of plural nouns—**regular** and **irregular**.

To form the plural of a regular noun, you add –*s* or –*es*. Some nouns change their spelling when you create the plural form.

> I have three different **rings** I like to wear.
> Usually, I keep them inside their **boxes**.
> I only take them out to wear them to **parties**.

Irregular plurals have their own unique spellings. It is best to memorize them or to use a dictionary to check their spelling.

> There were four **children** in the kitchen.
> The **women** of the early 1900s fought for the right to vote.
> Do you know the song "Three Blind **Mice**"?

Possessive Nouns are used to show ownership.

Add an apostrophe and an *s* to show the possessive of most singular nouns, even when the noun ends in an *s*.

> The music of the singer = The singer**'s** music
> The desk of the boss = The boss**'s** desk

Add only an apostrophe to show the possessive of plural nouns that end in *s* or *es*.

> The meeting of the coaches = The coaches**'** meeting

Add an apostrophe and an *s* in order to show the possessive of plural nouns that do not end in *s* or *es*.

> The whiteness of the teeth = The teeth**'s** whiteness

Contractions are shortened versions of words and phrases. Contractions are used more often in speech than in writing. They are formed by using apostrophes to show where the missing letters are located.

You can use a verb plus the word *not* to form a contraction.

> Ted and Mary **aren't** going to the soccer game today.
> They **couldn't** get a ride to the stadium.

You can use a pronoun plus the word *will* to form a contraction.

> **We'll** meet you outside the ticket booth.
> Do you think **you'll** be able to find us?

You can use a pronoun or noun plus the verb *be* to form a contraction.

> **Arlene's** saving seats for us.
> **She's** also going to get some popcorn for everyone.

You can use a pronoun or noun plus the verb *would* to form a contraction.

> **I'd** like to get there early to get a good seat.
> **Who'd** like to come with me?

Subject-Verb Agreement means that a verb must agree with its subject in number. You should make sure that both the subject and the verb are either singular or plural.

> INCORRECT: My sister run to the playground in the park.
> CORRECT: My sister **runs** to the playground in the park.

> INCORRECT: We moves back and forth in time to the music.
> CORRECT: We **move** back and forth in time to the music.

Pronoun Agreement Pronouns must agree with their *antecedents*, or the words they refer back to.

A personal pronoun must agree with its antecedent in person, number, and gender. *Person* means the person speaking, the person spoken to, or the person spoken about. *Number* means singular or plural. *Gender* means masculine or feminine.

> INCORRECT: Jonah told Daphne to bring a backpack with them.
> CORRECT: Jonah told Daphne to bring a backpack with **her**.

> INCORRECT: Travelers know that you can choose from many destinations.
> CORRECT: Travelers know that they can choose from many destinations.

Double Negatives A double negative is the use of two negative words in a sentence. Avoid double negatives. They change the meaning of the sentence.

> DOUBLE NEGATIVE: I don't have no more money.
> CORRECTION: I have no more money.

> DOUBLE NEGATIVE: No one did nothing about cleaning up.
> CORRECTION: No one did anything about cleaning up.

Irregular Verbs Many common verbs have unusual, or *irregular*, forms in the past tense. These verbs are irregular because they do not add *–ed* or *–d* to form the past tense.

© Harcourt

Sometimes, irregular verbs have the same past and past participle forms.

> PRESENT FORM: bring; pay; lose
>
> PAST FORM: brought; paid; lost
>
> PAST PARTICIPLE: (have) brought; (have) paid; (have) lost

Sometimes, irregular verbs have the same present, past, and past participle forms.

> PRESENT FORM: cost; hurt; put
>
> PAST FORM: cost; hurt; put
>
> PAST PARTICIPLE: (have) cost; (have) hurt; (have) put

Sometimes, irregular verbs have present, past, and past participle forms that change in other ways.

> PRESENT FORM: run; sing; wear
>
> PAST FORM: ran; sang; wore
>
> PAST PARTICIPLE: (have) run; (have) sung; (have) worn

Tricky Words

The meanings, sounds, and spelling of some words have to be memorized.

Homographs and Homophones **Homographs** are words that are spelled the same way but have different meanings. **Homophones** are words that sound the same, but they are spelled differently and have different meanings.

The italicized words in these sentences are spelled the same but have different meanings.

> HOMOGRAPHS: I felt *fine* today after I paid the overdue *fine* for my library book.
>
> HOMOGRAPHS: I can't *bear* to see another *bear* in this zoo.

The italicized words in these sentences sound the same but have different meanings and spellings.

> HOMOPHONES: I can't *bear* to feel too much sun on my *bare* arms.
>
> HOMOPHONES: Look over *there*. Ingrid and Maude are cooking *their* breakfast over a campfire. *They're* making scrambled eggs.

Spelling Tips

Some spelling words have to be memorized. Others follow patterns that can be applied to several different words.

Memorize words that are easily misspelled by keeping a list in a notebook. Learn their meanings to help you memorize how they are spelled.

> EASILY MISSPELLED WORDS: absence; aisle; calendar; curious; eighth; foreign; interfere; knowledge; nuisance; receipt; succeed; tomorrow

Plurals The plural form of most nouns is formed by adding –s or –es to the singular form.

> My new friend John brought his **friends** to my house.

For words that end in -s, -ss, -x, -z, -sh, or –ch, add –es to create the plural form.

> atlas; atlases
> compass; compasses
> fox; foxes
> waltz; waltzes
> match; matches

For words that end in –o preceded by a consonant, add either –es or –s to create the plural form.

> tomato; tomatoes
> piano; pianos

For words that end in –o preceded by a vowel, add –s to create the plural form.

> ratio; ratios

For words that end in –y preceded by a consonant, change the –y to an –i and add –es to create the plural form.

> party; parties

For words that end in –y preceded by a vowel, add –s to create the plural form.

> monkey; monkeys

For words that end in –f or –ff, add –s to create the plural form or change –f to –v and add –es to create the plural form.

> cliff; cliffs
> leaf; leaves

For words that end in –fe, change –f to –v and add –es to create the plural form.

> knife; knives

Prefixes The spelling of a word usually does not change when a prefix is added.

> *dis-* + appoint = disappoint
> *re-* + appear = reappear

Suffixes The spelling of some words changes when a suffix is added.

For words that end in *–y* preceded by a consonant, change the *–y* to an *–I* and add the suffix.

> **happy** changes to **happiness**

For words that end in *–y* preceded by a vowel, simply add the suffix.

> **enjoy** becomes **enjoyment**

When a suffix beginning with a vowel is added to a word that ends in *–e*, the *–e* is dropped when the suffix is added.

> **believe** becomes **believable**

When a suffix beginning with a consonant is added to a word that ends in *–e*, simply add the suffix.

> **price** becomes **priceless**

Spelling Rules help you learn a pattern that you can apply to several words.

The most famous spelling rule is "*i* before *e* except after *c*, or when sounded like *a*, as in *neighbor* and *weigh*."

> *ie* words: believe; siege
> *ei* words: deceive; receipt

There are some exceptions to this rule that must be memorized.

> leisure; foreign; their; weird

Proofreading Strategies

Written English follows certain **conventions,** or rules, that make it clear for readers. As you proofread, look for errors in your use of conventions. Once you have revised your writing to improve organization, tone, and word use, you can polish it in the proofreading stage.

Wait before proofreading. If you can, avoid proofreading your writing immediately. Set your draft aside, and return to it with a fresh eye.

Proofread in stages. You might want to follow these steps:
1. Read your composition for meaning. Notice whether you have indented paragraphs and whether your sentences make sense. Correct any fragments and run ons.
2. Next, look at grammar, usage, capitalization, and punctuation. Think about the rules you have learned, and apply them to your own writing.
3. Last, focus on spelling. Take the time to look up any words that might be misspelled in a dictionary.

Proofread with a partner. A classmate may see problems that you have overlooked.

 Technology

Keep track of your revisions. First, make a copy of your old file and rename it. For example, if your first draft is called Essay.doc, name the revised copy Essay2.doc. Revise the second copy. You can always open the old file to go back to your original version.

© Harcourt

Proofreading Checklist

This checklist will help you as you proofread your work.

Sentences and Paragraphs

☑ Does every sentence have a subject and a predicate?

☑ Have you used the correct form for compound and complex sentences?

☑ Have you indented each paragraph?

Grammar and Usage

☑ Do your verbs agree with their subjects?

☑ Have you used subject and object pronouns correctly?

☑ Have you used the correct form of adjectives and adverbs that compare?

Capitalization and Punctuation

☑ Have you capitalized proper nouns and the pronoun *I*?

☑ Have you used commas correctly in compound sentences, addresses, dates, and series of words?

☑ Have you used apostrophes correctly?

☑ Have you surrounded all direct quotations with quotation marks?

Spelling

☑ Are you sure of the spelling of every word?

ℓ	delete text
∧	insert text
↻	move text
¶	new paragraph
≡	capitalize
/	lowercase
◯	correct spelling

Technology

Remember that the computer spell checker won't catch homophone mistakes. The computer will think this sentence is correct: *Their is know weigh out.* The sentence actually should be *There is no way out.* Because the mistakes are in meaning rather than spelling, the computer won't help you find them.

© Harcourt

Presenting Your Work

Most writing is meant to reach an audience. The final writing stage is to publish your work, or present it to your readers. Here are some ideas that can help you connect your writing with your audience.

Publishing Ideas for Any Type of Writing

- Read it aloud.
- Place it in a class reading library or post it on a bulletin board.
- Have a partner read it silently.
- Send it to a friend as an e-mail attachment.

Publishing Ideas for Descriptive Writing

- Use music to enhance your writing. Record yourself reading to music.
- Take or find photographs to create an illustrated essay or magazine article.
- Use art materials to make a pictorial brochure.
- Make your writing the centerpiece of a collage, poster, or other artwork.

Strategies
Good Writers Use

- Think about your audience when making design decisions. Will illustrations or photographs help your readers understand your ideas?
- Try publishing one piece of work in two ways to see which method you think is more effective.

© Harcourt

Publishing Ideas for Narrative Writing

- Create an illustrated book for the classroom library.
- Direct a play or video based on your story.
- Share your story with students in another region by sending it as an e-mail attachment.
- Submit your writing to your school literary magazine.
- Enter your story in a writing contest.
- Include your story in a classroom anthology.

Publishing Ideas for Persuasive Writing

- Send your work as a letter to the editor of your school or local paper.
- Hold a classroom debate on the topic.
- Create a newsletter or pamphlet to distribute in your school or community.
- Give a speech to your class or to a school assembly.
- Post your work on your school's website.

Publishing Ideas for Expository Writing

- Collect class essays in an anthology with a broad topic, such as American history or biology.
- Make a poster for the school hallway.
- Use specialized software to create a multimedia report.
- Create a table display for the classroom or for a school fair.
- Take over as "teacher," and instruct your classmates.

Technology

If you are using a computer, print out one page of your final draft to review your font and spacing choices. Make sure that your fonts are easy to read. You might choose a bolder display font for the title.

Giving a Multimedia Presentation

Step 1

Reread your report. Choose information to show through photographs, a map, a poster, or other visual aids.

Step 2

Look in the library for audio or video recordings to accompany your report. Download from the Internet any images or sounds that you can use. Prepare any charts or graphs.

Step 3

Organize the equipment you need, such as a VCR, an audio player, or a computer.

Step 4

Plan and practice your presentation. Decide when to stop and what to show or play. Ask a classmate to assist you with equipment.

Step 5

Present your report with confidence. Speak loudly and clearly, looking at your audience. Answer questions at the end.

Strategies Good Writers Use

- Write legibly, or choose legible fonts.
- Leave adequate margins.
- Indent paragraphs.
- Put your name on your work.

© Harcourt

Strategies for Making an Oral Presentation	Applying the Strategies
Make note cards.	• Write each main idea with major details on a note card. Put your cards in order, and number them.
Use visual aids.	• Identify ideas to illustrate. Create pictures, charts, diagrams, music, video, or PowerPoint™ slides to add visual interest.
Practice.	• Practice in front of a mirror, a friend, or a family member, or tape your rehearsal. • Practice looking at your audience as you speak. Listeners will be more alert if you connect with them.
Present competently.	• Share your ideas with a firm and clear voice. Be prepared to answer questions from your audience.

Strategies for Listeners

- Identify the speaker's purpose, main idea, and point of view.

- Evaluate whether the speaker effectively supports the main idea.

- Determine if you agree with the speaker. What parts of the presentation do you like best? Which parts are less effective?

Writer's Glossary of Terms

adjective: a word that describes a noun

adverb: a word that describes a verb, an adjective, or another adverb

autobiographical composition: a composition that tells about an event or events in the writer's life

autobiographical narrative: the writer describes an event that happened in his or her life

biography: a factual account about a real person's life

cause-and-effect paragraph: a paragraph that tells about something that happens and why it happens

character description paragraph: a paragraph that gives a clear picture of what someone is like, usually using sensory details

compare-and-contrast essay: an essay that tells how things are alike and different

descriptive paragraph: a paragraph that tells what something or someone is like

detail: a fact, event, or statement; details usually tell abut a main idea

draft: a first attempt at a piece of writing

essay: a piece of writing that is not a story, usually with a clear purpose for writing

essay or explanation: an essay that tells how something is done, what something is like, or how to do something

fact: something that is true

how-to paragraph: a paragraph that tells how to do something

journal entry: a daily record of the writer's observations written in the first person

letter: a written message to someone

letter of request: a letter asking someone to do something

main idea: what something is mostly about

narrative composition: a story; some stories are fictional, with made-up characters, setting, and plot

narrative paragraph: a paragraph that tells a story

news article: a story about current events that appears or might appear in a newspaper

notes: writing that records facts or ideas from a source of information

outline: a system of organizing information and notes

paragraph: a group of sentences with a single main idea or topic

paragraph of explanation: a paragraph that tells how something works or how something is done

paragraph of historical information: a paragraph that presents facts and data

personal response paragraph: a paragraph in which the writer gives an opinion on a topic, supporting that opinion with facts and examples

persuasive letter: a letter that tries to convince someone to do something or to think a certain way

persuasive paragraph: a paragraph that tries to convince someone to do something or to think a certain way

poem: a piece of writing, often with rhyme

predicate: what the subject of a sentence does or is like

purpose for writing: the reason why someone writes something

reason: why something happens or is true

rhyme: a system of writing in which the sounds of words are alike, usually in a poem

rubric: a guide for scoring or evaluating something

sensory detail: a detail that "speaks" to one of the senses—sight, sound, touch, smell, or taste

sequence: the order in which things happen

skit: a short play using characters and dialogue to tell a story

story: a made-up tale

subject: what a sentence is about

summary: a short piece of writing that wraps up the main points of a longer piece of writing

suspense story: a mystery in which readers are not sure what will happen

topic: what something is about

verb: a word that names an action

	FOCUS/IDEAS	ORGANIZATION/PARAGRAPHS	DEVELOPMENT	VOICE	WORD CHOICE	SENTENCES	CONVENTIONS
Score of 4 ☆☆☆☆	The paper is completely focused on the task and has a clear purpose.	The paper has a clear beginning, middle, and ending. The ideas and details are presented in logical order. The writer uses transitions, such as *Finally, The next day,* or *However,* to show the relationships among ideas.	The paper has a clear central idea that is supported by strong specific details.	The writer's viewpoint is clear. The writer uses creative and original phrases and expressions where appropriate.	The writer uses clear, exact words and phrases. The writing is interesting to read.	The writer uses a variety of sentences. The writing flows smoothly.	There are few or no errors in grammar, punctuation, capitalization, and spelling.
Score of 3 ☆☆☆	The paper is generally focused on the task and the purpose.	The ideas and details are mostly presented in logical order. The writer uses some transitions to show the relationships among ideas.	The paper has a central idea and is supported by details.	The writer's viewpoint is somewhat clear. The writer uses some original phrases and expressions.	The word choices are clear. The writer uses some interesting words and phrases.	The writer uses some variety in sentences.	There are a few errors in grammar, punctuation, capitalization, and spelling.
Score of 2 ☆☆	The paper is somewhat focused on the task and purpose.	The organization is not clear in some places.	The paper does not have a clear central idea and has few supporting details.	The writer's viewpoint is unclear.	The writer does not use words or phrases that make the writing clear to the reader.	The writer does not use much variety in his or her sentences.	There are some errors in grammar, punctuation, capitalization, and spelling.
Score of 1 ☆	The paper does not have a clear focus or a purpose.	The paper has little or no organization.	The central idea is not clear and there are few or no supporting details.	The writer seems uninterested in what he or she is writing about.	The writer uses word choices that are unclear or inappropriate.	There is little or no variety in sentences. Some of the sentences are unclear.	There are many errors in grammar, punctuation, capitalization, and spelling.

Writer's Companion
Student Rubrics

		Score of 6	Score of 5	Score of 4	Score of 3	Score of 2	Score of 1
		☆☆☆☆☆☆	☆☆☆☆☆	☆☆☆☆	☆☆☆	☆☆	☆
FOCUS		The writing is completely focused on the topic and has a clear purpose.	The writing is focused on the topic and purpose.	The writing is generally focused on the topic and purpose.	The writing is somewhat focused on the topic and purpose.	The writing is related to the topic but does not have a clear focus.	The writing is not focused on the topic and purpose.
ORGANIZATION		The ideas in the paper are well-organized and presented in logical order. The paper seems complete to the reader.	The organization of the paper is mostly clear. The paper seems complete.	The organization is mostly clear, but the paper may seem unfinished.	The paper is somewhat organized, but seems unfinished.	There is little organization to the paper.	There is no organization to the paper.
SUPPORT		The writing has strong, specific details. The word choices are clear and fresh.	The writing has strong, specific details and clear word choices.	The writing has supporting details and some variety in word choice.	The writing has few supporting details. It needs more variety in word choice.	The writing uses few supporting details and very little variety in word choice.	There are few or no supporting details. The word choices are unclear.
CONVENTIONS		The writer uses a variety of sentences. There are few or no errors in grammar, spelling, punctuation, and capitalization.	The writer uses a variety of sentences. There are few errors in grammar, spelling, punctuation, and capitalization.	The writer uses some variety in sentences. There are a few errors in grammar, spelling, punctuation, and capitalization.	The writer uses simple sentences. There are some errors in grammar, spelling, punctuation, and capitalization.	The writer uses simple sentences. There are many errors in grammar, spelling, punctuation, and capitalization.	The writer uses unclear sentences. There are many errors in grammar, spelling, punctuation, and capitalization.